Killing for Religion

Killing for Religion

An Analysis of Conflict in Asia

Stephen R. Schwalbe

RESOURCE *Publications* • Eugene, Oregon

KILLING FOR RELIGION
An Analysis of Conflict in Asia

Copyright © 2022 Stephen R. Schwalbe. All rights reserved. Except for brief quotations in critical publications or reviews, no part of this book may be reproduced in any manner without prior written permission from the publisher. Write: Permissions, Wipf and Stock Publishers, 199 W. 8th Ave., Suite 3, Eugene, OR 97401.

Resource Publications
An Imprint of Wipf and Stock Publishers
199 W. 8th Ave., Suite 3
Eugene, OR 97401

www.wipfandstock.com

PAPERBACK ISBN: 978-1-6667-4310-4
HARDCOVER ISBN: 978-1-6667-4311-1
EBOOK ISBN: 978-1-6667-4312-8

MAY 24, 2022 12:55 PM

This book is dedicated to my wife, Ingrid, with all of my love

Contents

Figures | viii

Acknowledgements | ix

Abbreviations | x

CHAPTER 1	Introduction	1
CHAPTER 2	Violence and Conflict	8
CHAPTER 3	Hinduism	16
CHAPTER 4	Hinduism and Conflict	36
CHAPTER 5	Buddhism	44
CHAPTER 6	Buddhism and Conflict	80
CHAPTER 7	Shinto	97
CHAPTER 8	Shinto and Conflict	105
CHAPTER 9	Comparing Religions	112
CHAPTER 10	Comparing Religion and Conflict	126
CHAPTER 11	Conclusion	142

About the Author | 147

Bibliography | 149

Index | 155

Figures

1. Map of India
2. Indian Caste System
3. Map of China
4. Japanese Empire in 1942
5. Map of Southeast Asia
6. Venn Diagram of Selected Asian Religions

Acknowledgements

THIS BOOK COMPLETES a quest after discovering a gap in the literature regarding religion and conflict while teaching at the Air War College in 2007. It offers students and curious citizens a review and an assessment of conflict facilitated by the three largest Asian religions: Hinduism, Buddhism, and Shinto. It also reviews the related religious conflicts around Asia as well as identifies groups that are still propagating religious conflict.

I would like to thank Phillip Bernhardt-House for reviewing my manuscript and offering his keen insights, as well as my wife, Ingrid, for all her assistance and patience while I was researching and writing it.

Abbreviations

BBS	Bodu Bala Sena ("Buddhist Power Force")
BCE	Before the Common Era
BJP	Bharatiya Janata Party ("Indian People's Party")
CAB	Citizenship Amendment Bill
CE	Common Era
MaBa Tha	"Patriotic Association of Myanmar"
NEA	Northeast Asia
RSS	Rashtriya Swayamsevak Sangh ("National Volunteer Core")
SEA	Southeast Asia
ULC	Universal Life Church
UUC	Unitarian Universalist Church
WHO	World Health Organization

CHAPTER 1

Introduction

Some faiths every citizen should be acquainted with simply because hundreds of millions of people live by them.[1]

HUSTON SMITH, 1991

MOST OF THE U.S. military personnel stationed or deployed overseas in Asia are not aware of how the religions in Asia facilitate conflict. (In fact, most Americans are probably not aware of this as well.[2]) For the tens of thousands of members of the U.S. Armed Forces providing security in Asia today, it would be useful for them to know what they might be fighting for or against, especially if it has to do with religious beliefs (such as those evident in Muslim terrorist attacks). For American taxpayers, it may be important to know this as well considering the exorbitant national costs involved.

For example, Shinto is the native religion of Japan and is oriented around nature. As such, it is very peaceful and serene. However, in the early half of the 20th century, the Japanese emperor weaponized Shinto and recast it into "State Shinto." All assets of the Shinto religion became government property, and all *Kannushi* (Shinto priests) were required to work for the Department of Shinto. Soon, the Japanese Imperial Army and Navy were directed to prepare and conduct "special" (i.e., suicide) missions

---

1. Smith, *The World's Religions*, 3.
2. Only about a third of Americans polled in 2010 could identify key characteristics about either Hinduism or Buddhism. https://www.pewforum.org/2010/09/28/u-s-religious-knowledge-survey-who-knows-what-about-religion/#World

sanctioned by State Shinto. As such, in 1944 when the War in the Pacific turning against it, Japan launched numerous special *kamikaze* flights (suicide missions) into U.S. and allied naval ships, including aircraft carriers such as the USS *Franklin*. Close to 20 percent of the kamikaze attacks were successful, killing more than seven thousand U.S. naval personnel.

Today, with around 50,000 military forces in Japan stationed among 23 bases; 28,500 military forces in South Korea stationed among 18 bases; and 5,000 military forces in Guam stationed at two strategic bases, the United States is heavily invested in the international security of Asia.[3] With the growing hostility demonstrated by China, this American military force posture is likely to grow in this region in the near future.

Despite the international perception that Asian religions, such as Buddhism and Shinto, are inherently peaceful, there are many religious conflicts on-going in Asia today. The most prevalent one is the persecution of over one million Rohingya Muslims by the Buddhist government of Myanmar (formerly known as Burma). The United Nations has even launched a genocide investigation against the Myanmar government regarding its persecution of the Rohingya people.[4] As well, one of the most dangerous conflicts in Asia is over the Kashmir region of northern India. It is a conflict between the Hindu-dominant Indian government and the Muslim-dominant Pakistani government, with both governments claiming the area (as well as against the Chinese who also claim some of the area). Well before the partition of India into two nations – India and Pakistan, Hindus and Muslims had been fighting one another across southern Asia for over a thousand years. The primary purpose of this book, then, is to discuss three primary Asian religions and how they accommodate and justify violence and conflict so that Westerners might gain some insights as to why these conflicts have occurred, are occurring, and likely will continue to occur.

Criteria

There are many religions in Asia. However, analyzing all of them here would be impractical. As such, I will focus on three major religions; specifically,

---

3. https://theworld.org/stories/2017-08-11/us-has-massive-military-presence-asia-pacific-heres-what-you-need-know-about-it

4. https://apnews.com/article/crime-myanmar-united-nations-c8d30050193ccc2aff-c15c508ee4be3d

Introduction

those Asian religions that rank in the top ten religions in the world by the number of adherents. To begin, we can rule out the three Abrahamic religions, i.e., Judaism, Christianity, and Islam, as they are not generally considered Asian religions. I also wanted to consider key countries in the region as another criterion. The criteria regarding key countries include those with American forces present in them; those involved in a religious conflict at some point in their history; or those with significant geopolitical influence today. Eligible countries would include Japan, South Korea, China, India, and Thailand.

As such, the first Asian religion I selected is Hinduism, which has over a billion followers primarily resident in India. Hinduism has been the third largest religion in the world for many years. The next selection is Buddhism, the fourth largest religion in the world with around a half a billion followers. Buddhism began in India and still has a large presence there with over eight million adherents. While it was a major religion in China in the past, China still has over two hundred and forty-four million Buddhist citizens today – the most in any one country in the world. Buddhism is also a major influence in Japan. As well, Buddhism is prevalent in many Southeast Asian countries, including Sri Lanka, Myanmar, and Thailand. Shinto is the final Asian religion selected. It is the fifth largest religion in the world with around 100 million followers, primarily resident in Japan.

All three of these selected religions have witnessed conflict in the recent past. As well, there are many American military bases in Japan – but, none in India or China. Of the three selected religions, only Buddhism is considered a "global" religion, such as Christianity and Islam, though it is present primarily in Asia, hence, more of a regional religion.

Audience

The intended audience for this book includes primarily the members of the U.S. Armed Forces that are stationed or deployed to countries in the Far East to keep the peace and be ready to fight. It should be important to each member of the U.S. Armed Services how religion affects conflict that the United States may become involved in. As well, American citizens as taxpayers may want to know more about the religions facilitating conflicts in the Far East.

Many of the topics of this book could fill up an entire book in and of themselves. For example, there are many millions of Hindu deities, but I will only review the most important ones. This caveat applies primarily to the definitions of Hinduism, Buddhism, and Shinto. I will review the key aspects of each of these religions so that an analysis (i.e., compare and contrast) can be conducted with the Abrahamic religions, specifically regarding violence and conflict.

In the academic world, whenever a reader sees "vs" in the text, the author is about to compare and contrast two concepts – in other words, provide some analysis. Analysis is one of the more challenging aspects of academia because it is not always easy to do. This book is a collection of many of the best sources available on the topic of religion and conflict in Asia, saving readers a lot of time and effort to research it for themselves.

Author

It is important for any author to reveal any personal biases when offering such a book to readers. One reason I feel qualified to write on this subject is that I have no religious preferences or biases. I have never belonged to a specific church or religion. My mother was Catholic while my father was Protestant. As such, one might classify me as an agnostic, not wanting to pick one religion (and, hence, one parent) over the other.

Another reason I am interested in this topic is because of my thirty-year career as an officer in the Air Force. I represented the U.S. Air Force in two assignments as a Defense Attaché – in South Korea (a Buddhist country) and then in Jordan (a Muslim country). As such, conflicts, war, the U.S. Air Force, and Northeast Asia are a few areas of my expertise and interest.

Structure

With the Asian religions selected and the audience and author identified, let me discuss the structure of this book. First, it is important to analyze what constitutes a religion as the Asian religions have little in common with the Abrahamic religions that Westerners are familiar with. Once this is done, I will define each of the three Asian religions selected: Hinduism, Buddhism, and Shinto (in that order throughout the book). With the insights into the basics of these three Asian religions, it would be useful to compare them with each other as well as with the three Abrahamic religions to better understand the Asian religions and their commonalities with the Western religions.

To prepare for the discussion about religion and conflict in Asia, we need to discuss how each of these three religions allows for violence and conflict. After that is completed, I will analyze the nature of religious conflict within the Asian religions as compared to the nature of religious conflict within the Abrahamic religions. So, let's begin with a definition of a religion.

Definitions of Religion

There are many definitions of religion, so for this study, let me define it as a collection of beliefs within a cultural system that relates mankind to a higher order of existence as well as the spiritual practice of these beliefs. According to Charles Selengut, professor of sociology at Drew University, religions "promulgate a divine view of the moral and social order that they take to be binding on all humanity."[5] At this point, it would be good to note that as of 2015, *84 percent* of the world's population identified themselves with at least one religious group.[6]

Macro Level

At a macro level, a couple of fundamental purposes of having religion are that it gives people hope and comfort. These aspects are crucial for people's mental health regarding present day challenges and what happens to them after death. It also provides social order, which is a sense of belonging and connection among citizens in society. This is accomplished through individuals, families, schools, public organizations, the workplace, and religious organizations.

Religion has evolved throughout human history from dominating early societies to becoming more of a spiritual hobby in the modern world. Huston Smith, a renowned historian of religion who taught at Washington University and the University of California at Berkeley, observed that

---

5. Selengut, *Sacred Fury*, 2.
6. Sherwood, "Religion: Why faith is becoming more and more popular," https://www.theguardian.com/news/2018/aug/27/religion-why-is-faith-growing-and-what-happens-next

"for the bulk of human history, religion was lived in a tribal and virtually timeless mode."[7] However, with the scientific progress of the past couple of centuries, religion has moved from the center of society dictating policy to the boundaries of society offering guidance on policy.

The global religions, such as Christianity, Islam, and Buddhism, tend to mix their basic tenets with one another as well as with local religions. This concept is known as syncretism.[8] Smith noted that "Every religion mixes universal principles with local peculiarities."[9] Regarding religion's messaging, Smith concluded that "Religion is not primarily a matter of facts, it is a matter of meanings."[10] Many people look to religious myths for meaning to help them cope with life. Selengut found that "a myth helps people make sense of life; it is certainly not to be taken as literally true."[11] Others believe religion is merely an instrument used to expand one's own power.[12]

Religion also reflects the cultural values of society. However, it is difficult to compromise regarding values. When mixing religious beliefs of society with the political goals of the elites, conflict inevitably results. Finally, religion can radicalize conflicts, resulting in a zero-sum situation and increasing the willingness to fight.[13]

Micro Level

The Abrahamic religions (Judaism, Christianity, Islam) set the world standard for what is expected in a "robust" religion. Most religions believe in a supreme deity. This concept is known as "theism." So, a belief in just one god is monotheism, while a belief in multiple gods is polytheism.[14] Each of the Abrahamic religions is fairly monotheistic, be it God or Allah.

Each also has a primary prophet (also known as messenger), from Judaism's Moses in the Torah (Hebrew Bible) to Christianity's Jesus in the New Testament of the Bible, to Islam's Prophet Muhammad in the *Qur'an*. Each of these religions also has its own primary sacred text indirectly

---

7. Smith, *The World's Religions*, xiii.
8. Syncretism is the amalgamation of different religions.
9. Smith, *The World's Religions*, 3.
10. Smith, *The World's Religions*, 3.
11. Selengut, *Sacred Fury*, 67.
12. Von de Waals, *The Rohingya in Myanmar*, 6.
13. Von de Waals, *The Rohingya in Myanmar*, 6.
14. Parrinder, *World's Religions*, 15.

Introduction

transmitted to humankind from God or Allah. These books provide written legitimacy to their respective religions. They include the Hebrew Bible for Judaism; the Holy Bible for Christianity; and the *Qur'an* for Islam.

Each of these religions has a weekly worship tradition. In Judaism, congregations of Jewish faithful gather weekly around Saturday in synagogues to participate in communal prayer, singing, and learning. In Christianity, each weekly church service on Sundays normally features a Eucharist ceremony (also known as Holy Communion) reenacting the Last Supper in remembrance of Jesus Christ's sacrifice during Passover. In Islam, in addition to praying five times every day while facing Mecca, Saudi Arabia, Muslims congregate to pray together, usually led by an Imam, on Fridays.

Each religion has a rite of passage to become a member. To become a Jew, one must appeal to a rabbi at least three times to convert to Judaism. Once a person has a rabbi's support, that person must successfully pass a Jewish council interview about Jewish history, culture, and traditions. Finally, all male candidates must be properly circumcised. To become Christian, one must only be baptized. This ritual involves a priest sprinkling or pouring water on the candidate's head or immersing the person's body in water, as John the Baptist did with Jesus. Finally, in Islam one only needs to recite one time, sincerely, in Arabic, the belief in the oneness of Allah and acceptance of Muhammad as Allah's messenger (aka prophet). This testimony is known as *Shahada* in Arabic and serves as one of the five pillars of Islam.

Religions often have an attachment to specific territory. For Judaism, God promised land to the Jewish people for eternity. In *Exodus* 23:31, the borders of this Holy Land were described as "from the sea of reeds (i.e., the Red Sea) to the Sea of Philistines (i.e., the Mediterranean Sea), and from the desert to the Euphrates River." For Christians, the Holy Land consists of the land between the Jordan River and the Mediterranean Sea, including the biblical land of Israel and the region of Palestine. For Islam, it has two holy cities (where the Prophet Mohammad lived), Mecca and Medina in Saudi Arabia, and the al-Aqsa Mosque on the Temple Mount in Jerusalem.

CHAPTER 2

Violence and Conflict

Warfare is an intrinsic part of being human. War isn't a modern invention, but an ancient, fundamental part of our humanity. Historically, all peoples warred. Our oldest writings are filled with war stories. Archeology reveals ancient fortresses and battles, and sites of prehistoric massacres going back millennia.[1]

RYUSAKU TSUNODA, 1958

War and politics are the venues for religious battles.[2]

CHARLES SELENGUT, 2003

God is the cause of evil.[3]

NICHOLAS GIER, 2014

THIS CHAPTER WILL COVER the sources of violence and conflict within the Asian religions.

---

1. De Bary ed., *Sources of Japanese Tradition*, 1.
2. Selengut, *Sacred Fury*, 152.
3. Gier, *The Origins of Religious Violence*, 249.

Violence

Violence is the use of physical force at a micro, individual level to injure, damage, or destroy. The World Health Organization (WHO) divides violence into 3 broad categories: 1) self-directed violence; 2) interpersonal violence; and 3) collective violence.[4] The analysis in this book only deals with *collective violence* that is committed to advance a particular agenda, in this case, a religious cause. Mary Jackman, a professor at the University of California at Davis, defined violence as encompassing "actions that inflict, threaten, or cause injury." Such actions may be "corporal, written, or verbal," and the injuries may be "corporal, psychological, material, or social."[5] The violence most applicable to this analysis is that which inflicts physical injury or death upon another person(s).[6]

Violence is part of human nature.[7] (The Latin root of violence is *violare* – a violation of another.[8]) Regarding the relevance of violence in Asia, Kaushik Roy, a professor at Jadavpur University in Calcutta, India, assessed that "For non-Western societies, violence remains the moral essence of the warrior. Violence is existential."[9] As well, most Asians throughout history found that being a warrior was superior to being a farmer who worked the land.[10]

When analyzing religious violence, there are many other aspects to consider as well. John Hall, a professor of sociology at the University of California at Davis, noted that religious violence is embedded in moments of history and structures of culture.[11] This perspective indicates that such violence changes over time by necessity.[12] How societies view violence can alter as a result of changes in the environment or leadership. Threats may evolve leading to violence. Technology evolves, often facilitating violence. Charles Selengut, a professor of sociology at County College of Morris,

---

4. Violence Prevention Alliance, https://www.who.int/violenceprevention/approach/definition/en/
5. Lehr, *Militant Buddhism*, 17.
6. Jerryson and Juergensmeyer eds., *Buddhist Warfare*, 6.
7. Selengut, *Sacred Fury*, 50.
8. Jerryson, *Buddhist Fury*, 13.
9. Roy, *Hinduism and the Ethics of Warfare in South Asia*, 4.
10. Armstrong, *Fields of Blood*, 32. As well, for thousands of years, the warrior caste was always higher than the farmer/landowner/merchant caste.
11. Hall, *Religion and Violence*, 9.
12. Lehr, *Militant Buddhism*, 46.

explained that "Each civilization is anchored in its unique religious worldview, history, and moral system and has an attachment to land and territory it considers sacred and divinely set aside for it."[13] Selengut cited the following land as examples of sacred territory worth fighting for: "mother India," Kashmir, Israel, and Kosovo.[14]

Religious violence is also employed differently in different circumstances. Many times, such violence is justified as the last resort.[15] In other cultures, it is the ends that justify the means.[16] In any case, in religious conflict, each side claims it has a sacred obligation to wage war against the other side.[17] (Holy War lies in the eye of the beholder![18]) Religious leaders cite selective sacred scripture and one's religious duty to prosecute Holy Wars.[19] Both sides perceive themselves as threatened by the other side, hence, are the righteous defenders fighting for a just cause. Moreover, regarding perceived threats, there are no permanent friends, just permanent enemies.[20] As a result, the faithful are offered a difficult choice; if you are a true believer and wish to remain a part of the community, you must concur with the injunction to wage violence against the religion's enemies.[21] Gier noted a related irony stating, "those who worshipped the highest good would tend to commit more violence and be more intolerant than those who do not have such a moral focus."[22]

Usually, it is when religion gets involved in state affairs that violence is most likely to occur. Once a state government or king invokes religious motivation, then conflict against the state or kingdom becomes a sacred endeavor.[23] Nicholas Gier, a professor of philosophy at the University of Idaho, concluded that whenever religious and national identities are fused, one will find religiously-motivated violence, and this is true for all

---

13. Selengut, *Sacred Fury*, 142.
14. Selengut, *Sacred Fury*, 143.
15. Lehr, *Militant Buddhism*, 74.
16. Selengut, *Sacred Fury*,144.
17. Selengut, *Sacred Fury*, 3.
18. Lehr, *Militant Buddhism*, 249.
19. Selengut, *Sacred Fury*, 17.
20. Roy, *Hinduism and the Ethics of Warfare in South Asia*, 255.
21. Selengut, *Sacred Fury*, 8.
22. Gier, *The Origins of Religious Violence*, 241.
23. Hall, *Religion and Violence*, 10.

religions.[24] Moreover, Gier found that religious syncretism was more common in Asian religions than with Abrahamic religions.[25] And, because most religions are syncretic, this can lead to followers believing their religion is superior to others. This superiority complex leads to intolerance towards other religions that often leads to religious conflict.[26]

In most Asian religions, just war theory is known as *Dharmayuddha*.[27] *Dharmayuddha* is a Sanskrit word made up of two roots: *dharma*—meaning righteousness, and *yuddha*—meaning warfare. A key characteristic of the *Dharmayuddha* is that violence is justified as the last resort; after peaceful methods of conflict resolution have failed.[28] This theory is founded on *Hisma* – the doctrine of violence (conversely, *Ahisma* is the doctrine of non-violence).[29] With regard to *Hisma* and *Ahisma*, religion is one of the few forces throughout human history to both facilitate and mitigate violence.[30] Samuel Huntington, a professor at Harvard University, claimed that "[R]eligion was the central force that motivates and mobilizes people."[31] Mark Juergensmeyer, a professor of Sociology and Global Studies at the University of California at Santa Barbara, concluded that there was a "dark attraction" between religion and violence as reflected in the myths and legends of war, sacrifice, and martyrdom inherent within all great religious traditions.[32] Finally, turning to Asia, Marc Gopin, a professor at Tufts University, found that "Many violent trends are initiated in India with various radical Hindu parties' use of sacred mythic tales of the gods, using the dramas of defeat and victory to stir up rage against foreigners and specifically Muslims."[33] Such violence is important in sacred stories.[34]

---

24. Gier, *The Origins of Religious Violence*, 252.
25. Gier, *The Origins of Religious Violence*, 19.
26. Gier, *The Origins of Religious Violence*, 246.
27. Roy, *Hinduism and the Ethics of Warfare in South Asia*, xiii.
28. Rambachan, "The Coexistence of Violence and Nonviolence in Hinduism," 98.
29. Roy, *Hinduism and the Ethics of Warfare in South Asia*, xi.
30. Smith, *The World's Religions*, 10; Selengut, *Sacred Fury*, 50.
31. Huntington, *The Clash of Civilizations*, 27.
32. Juergensmeyer, Kitts, and Jerryson, eds., *Violence and the World's Religious Traditions*, 1–2.
33. Gopin, *Between Eden and Armageddon*, 14.
34. Gopin, *Between Eden and Armageddon*, 9.

Conflict

Conflict in this analysis is the physical violence at the macro level, involving groups of people, either as a nation-state or followers of a particular religion. Conflict can range from a duel to a battle to a war. Armed conflict is often characterized as war, a state of prolonged large-scale battle involving two or more groups of people, usually under the auspices of a government. Michael Jerryson, a professor of religious studies at Youngstown State University, defined warfare as "the processes and activities associated with war specifically for defeating an enemy or territorial conquest. They can manifest in the spiritual dimension as well."[35] In fact, physical violence and warfare are the more identified forms of conflict.[36] For example, Plato considered war as a necessity.[37] Aristotle believed war was justified—when it was in self-defense. According to Karen Armstrong, a prolific British author on religion, "War is an enticing elixir. It allows us to be noble. Still, we fight. But, to bring ourselves to do so, we envelop the effort in a mythology – often a religious mythology. We are fighting for God and country or that a particular war is 'just' or 'legal.'"[38]

While warfare was common in ancient times, it was often necessary to raise funds to conduct the fight as well as to profit from it, and it often contained a religious aspect to legitimize it.[39] Moreover, in ancient times, there was no difference between government and religion – religious leaders led most societies.[40] Ancient philosophers attempted to make the distinction between just and unjust wars, however, they never questioned the legitimacy of such violence.[41] Rory Cox, professor of history at the University of Saint Andrews, wrote in a 2017 study that the *just war* tradition can be traced as far back as to ancient Egypt.[42] Saint Augustine, Bishop of Hippo Regius in Numidia (Roman North Africa) at the end of the Roman Empire (5th Century CE), attempted to justify and condone religious warfare with

---

35. Jerryson and Juergensmeyer, *Buddhist Warfare*, 6.
36. Jerryson, *Buddhist Fury*, 13.
37. Tikhonov and Brekke, eds., *Buddhism and Violence*, 4.
38. Armstrong, *Fields of Blood*, 11.
39. Armstrong, *Fields of Blood*, 36, 43.
40. Armstrong, *Fields of Blood*, 15.
41. Tikhonov and Brekke, eds., *Buddhism and Violence*, 4.
42. Cox, "Expanding the History of the Just War: The Ethics of War in Ancient Egypt," 371.

his theory of Righteous War or Just War.[43] He believed there were legitimate reasons for conducting warfare, including defending or proselytizing religion.[44] His theory of Just War included two primary aspects: *Jus ad Bellum* – the right to go to war; and, *Jus in Bello* – the right conduct during war.[45]

Most polytheistic religions in the world (those having multiple gods, such as Hinduism and Shinto) include a god of war.[46] Despite these war deities, when religion causes conflict, it goes counter to what most people believe religion stands for – peace and goodwill. The bottom line is that conflict is found in all religions, including the Asian religions.[47]

Most ancient battles used religion to justify conflict. According to Peter Lehr, a professor of international relations at the University of Saint Andrews, "Hinduism, Buddhism, and Zen Buddhism have now incorporated elements of holy war in their religious outlook."[48] These ancient battles were perceived as part of a Holy War being fought between good and evil.[49] Selengut identified three general characteristics of Holy War to include: 1) defending one's religion; 2) ensuring religious conformity; and 3) following a charismatic religious leader.[50]

Often, it was easier to fight and kill the enemy when told they were demonic or not human. Lehr confirmed this writing, "Another possibility to justify war is to demonize or 'othering' of the enemy – a practice well known and practiced across all cultures and times."[51] This occurred most often when Asian religions were fighting against Muslims.[52]

Throughout Asian history, there have been many empires that were built, expanded, and destroyed by war, including the Akkadian, Sumerian, Babylonian, Assyrian, Macedonian, Roman, Mongol, and Ottoman Empires. A couple of the more famous Asian warriors included Genghis Khan and Indian King Prithviraja III. Note that the threat to a religion

43. Lehr, *Militant Buddhism*, 68.
44. Lehr, *Militant Buddhism*, 70.
45. Lehr, *Militant Buddhism*, 71.
46. Tikhonov and Brekke, eds., *Buddhism and Violence*, 2–3.
47. Juergensmeyer, Kitts, and Jerryson, *Violence and the World's Religious Traditions*, 3.
48. Lehr, *Militant Buddhism*, 18.
49. Tikhonov and Brekke, eds., *Buddhism and Violence*, 4.
50. Selengut, *Sacred Fury*, 22.
51. Lehr, *Militant Buddhism*, 71.
52. Lehr, *Militant Buddhism*, 232.

or an empire is more often from another religion or empire. However, it can also be from within a religion or empire. Scholars, such as Peter Lehr and Kaushik Roy, point out that in Holy Wars, any internal threat is *more* dangerous to the ruling regime than an external one.[53] Internal threats can evolve into religious civil wars which are more destructive, cause more deaths, and last a lot longer than non-religious wars.[54]

According to Selengut's third characteristic of Holy War, a strong charismatic leader championing a religious tradition has normally been required to trigger religious conflict. According to Gabriel Almond, a professor of political science at Stanford University, "Male charismatic or authoritarian leaders emerged from each religious tradition . . . New fundamentalist leaders ransack a tradition's past, retrieving and restoring politically useful doctrines and practices and creating others to construct an ideology capable of mobilizing youth into militant cadres."[55] Charismatic leaders are often skilled at manipulating sacred texts to serve their political goals.[56]

In ancient times, charismatic leaders were often kings. Vladimir Tikhonov, a professor at Oslo University, noted that the "Chinese placed warmaking as just part of kingship's routine. War was in the normal order of things . . . Religion not only sanctioned the violence, it also sacralized it."[57] According to the Buddhist sacred text, the *Lotus Sutra*,

> "A powerful king,
> Gives as rewards to his soldiers,
> Who have distinguished themselves in battle."[58]

Recently, we have seen charismatic leaders leading fundamentalist religious groups, particularly terrorist groups, such as al-Qaeda's Osama bin Laden. Almond characterized this stating, "The typical form of fundamentalist organizations is charismatic, a leader-follower relationship in which the

---

53. Lehr, *Militant Buddhism*, 18; Roy, *Hinduism and the Ethics of Warfare in South Asia*, 138.

54. Roy, *Hinduism and the Ethics of Warfare in South Asia*, 249.

55. Almond, Appleby, and Sivan. *Strong Religion*, 10.

56. Almond, Appleby, and Sivan. *Strong Religion*, 14.

57. Tikhonov and Brekke, eds., *Buddhism and Violence*, 2.

58. Shinozaki, Ziporyn, and David Earhart. Translators. *The Threefold Lotus Sutra*, 257.

follower imputes extraordinary qualities and special access to the deity. One man set apart from the others."[59]

Within the Asian religions, conflict is justified in highly theoretical and assumptive ways. If the soul does not exist or cannot be killed, then no one can really be killed.[60] If everyone is going to be reincarnated, then they can never really be permanently dead. As such, killing becomes inconsequential. According to Paul Demieville, former co-editor of the *T'oung Pao* – the oldest international journal of sinology, "There is no more existence than non-existence, no more life than death."[61] As well, killing to prevent crime or others from being killed is considered an act of charity and compassion, therefore, a good thing.[62]

Now that we have generically explored violence and conflict concerning religion, let us turn our attention to the basic tenets of each of the Asian religions selected before discussing how they accommodate conflict, beginning with Hinduism.

---

59. Almond, Sivan, and Appleby, *Strong Religion*, 98.
60. Tikhonov and Brekke, eds., *Buddhism and Violence*, 196.
61. Almond, Sivan, and Appleby, *Strong Religion*, 44.
62. Juergensmeyer, Kitts, and Jerryson, *Violence and the World's Religious Traditions*, 69.

Chapter 3

Hinduism

HINDUISM IS THE OLDEST religion in the world, going back at least five thousand years. It is an "eternal" religion with continuous cycles of life, death, and rebirth.[1] It is the most prevalent religion in India, which has more religious groups than most other countries in the world, including eight major religions. While Hinduism is not the official state religion, around 80 percent of India consists of Hindu citizens.[2] India officially defines a Hindu as an Indian who is not a Muslim, Christian, or Jewish.[3] Hinduism is perceived by Indians themselves as a traditional way of life and not necessarily a religion.[4] In India, there is no ethnic unity, no religious unity, and no consensus on what it is to be Hindu.[5] According to Anantanand Rambachan, a professor of religion, philosophy and Asian studies at Saint Olaf College, "Hinduism does not have a central institutional structure, a single sacred book, or uniform and required beliefs and rituals. The name 'Hindu' is itself an inclusive one that describes the indigenous traditions of India, a compendium of doctrinal and ritual diversity. Hinduism has never been a monolith."[6] Hindus believe that all

---

1. Langley, *World Religions*, 18.
2. Only 43 countries (22% of all countries) have official state religions. Far more countries, 116 (or 58%), have no official state religion according to the PEW Research Center.
3. Parrinder, *World Religions*, 192. India is a multi-lingual, multi-ethnic, and multi-religious society in southern Asia.
4. Doniger, *On Hinduism*, 8. Hinduism does not satisfy the traditional features of a religion. It is a way of life.
5. Cook, *Ancient Religions, Modern Politics*, 120.
6. Rambachan, "The Coexistence of Violence and Nonviolence in Hinduism," 98.

Asian religions are part of, or emanate from, Hinduism.⁷ For example, Gandhi believed Buddhism and Jainism were the same as Hinduism.⁸

Hinduism is the primary religion in India and Nepal, with a significant presence in Indonesia (see map of India). There are over 1.3 billion Hindus (about 15 percent of the world's population), making it the third largest religion in the world today after Christianity and Islam.

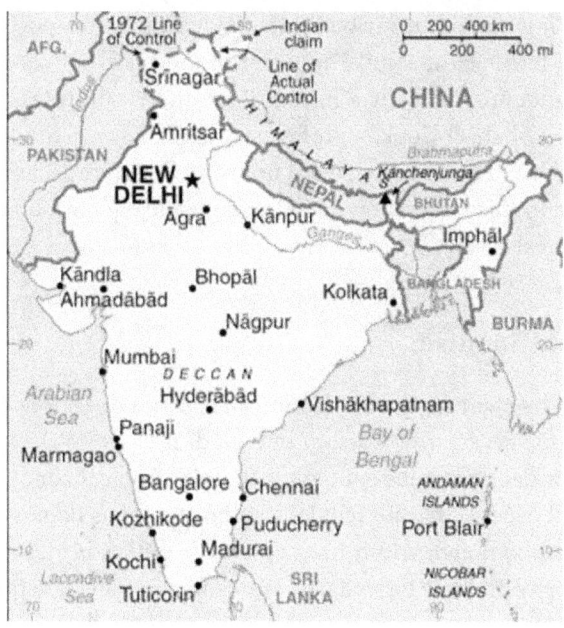

Map of India⁹

Hindu

The term "Hindu" does not emanate from a religion but from geography – referencing the Aryan ("noble") people who dominated northern India with their horses and horse-drawn carriages from 1800-1400 BCE.¹⁰ (The

---

7. Gier, *The Origins of Religious Violence*, 26.
8. Gier, *The Origins of Religious Violence*, 57.
9. CIA World Factbook, https://engineering.purdue.edu/~shripad/CIA%20--%20The%20World%20Factbook%20--%20India.htm
10. Olivelle, *Upanishad*, xxi.

alternative native word for Indians is Aryans.[11]) Note that Hindus do not define themselves by geography, but by their practices.[12] The word itself (and its derivative "Hinduism") is derived from the Persian language, not Hindi, Urdu, or Sanskrit.[13]

With the influx of British and other European merchants in the 18th century, foreigners began referring to the adherents of Indian religion collectively as "Hindus." After the British colonized India, they began to classify the population in various ways, including by religion. The British adopted the terms Hindu and Hinduism in the early 19th century.[14] However, Hindu identity is really a fusion of ethnicity, culture, and religion.[15] According to Michael Cook, a professor of Near Eastern Studies at Princeton University, "Hindu heritage did not fit well with the liberal view"[16] as nothing in Hinduism accommodates freedom and equality. Finally, Hindus are a patrilineal society.[17]

Aspects of Hinduism

Let us begin by identifying what Hinduism is *not*. It does not have a prophet; it does not necessarily worship one God; it does not have a primary holy book; it does not believe in any one philosophical concept; it has no ecclesiastical order; it has no religious authority; it has no governing body (i.e., it is autonomous); and it has no general initiation rituals. However, Hindus do pray multiple times a day, more often in the home than at a local temple.[18]

The operative ideologies for most Hindu practitioners include: 1) proper goals in life (*dharma*); 2) prosperity/work; 3) desires/passions; 4) freedom from rebirth/salvation; 5) karma (action/intent/consequences); 6) the cycle of death and rebirth; and 7) a path to attain *Moshka* (akin to

---

11. Olivelle, *Upanishad*, xxi.
12. Cook, *Ancient Religions, Modern Politics*, 57.
13. Cook, *Ancient Religions*, 409; Doniger, *On Hinduism*, 8; Langley, *World Religions*, 19.
14. However, Europeans did not invent the Hindu religion as is commonly thought.
15. Cook, *Ancient Religions, Modern Politics*, 73.
16. Cook, *Ancient Religions, Modern Politics*, 195.
17. Cook, *Ancient Religions, Modern Politics*, 196.
18. Parrinder, *World Religions*, 194, 212.

Nirvana).[19] Hinduism's eternal duties include honesty, patience, compassion, self-restraint, and not injuring or killing any living being. Killing an animal or human *under any circumstance* is a serious offense that will result in rebirth as a lower organism.[20] This is because Hindus believe that all living creatures have an internal, eternal soul known as *Atman*.[21] Hinduism is about understanding Brahman,[22] the transcendent oneness of all things, from within your *Atman*. Moreover, *Moksha* is the most important goal in Hinduism. It is the liberation from sorrow, suffering, and the endless cycle of rebirth. It entails self-realization that brings a state of bliss and ever-lasting happiness. According to Cook, "The essence of Hinduism comes from the Vedas, hostility to killing cows, veneration of Ram, monasteries, pilgrimages, and Muslims being its historic enemy."[23] Given the many people living in India relative to other regions of the world, it is not surprising that in Hinduism, mankind is immersed in a collective conscience—in stark contrast to the individual conscience of the West.[24]

The most rigorous practice of Hinduism takes place among monks and renunciates who live ascetic lives.[25] The praying and meditating occurs most often in monasteries and at temples. A Hindu temple is a sacred place where humans and gods come together in prayer. Eastern religions, in general, encourage asceticism and self-mortification as a means of purification.[26] Because of the plurality of doctrinal schools within Hinduism, it is often considered a range of religions, not just one.

Finally, the Vedic tradition is one where the rajas (kings) governed society while relying on the Brahmins (priestly caste) for legitimacy in return for guarantees of safety and material resources.[27] However, with its independence from Great Britain, India has legally become a secular society. The 42nd Amendment of the Constitution of India enacted in 1976 even

---

19. Nalini, *Hinduism*, 1.
20. Parrinder, *World Religions*, 211.
21. Huston Smith, *The World's Religions*, 66.
22. Also referred to as Brahma.
23. Cook, *Ancient Religions, Modern Politics*, 70.
24. Panikkar, *Hinduism*, 67fn.
25. Cook, *Ancient Religions, Modern Politics*, 194.
26. Selengut, *Sacred Fury*, 184. Hinduism has high regard for elective poverty—not involuntary poverty. (Cook, *Ancient Religions, Modern Politics*, 194).
27. Vaishnav, "Religious Nationalism and India's Future," 2.

asserts that India is a secular nation. The Constitution does not permit the mixing of religion and state power. However, the separation of church and state as we know it in the West is not the same in India. The Western concept of secularism does not believe in an open display of religion except for places of worship—which is not the same in India.[28] Hinduism remains the essence of daily life in India.

Dharma

Dharma, mentioned earlier, is a Sanskrit word that represents a concept of religious living in India. There are no good translations for the word *dharma* in Western languages. The concept of *dharma* was already in use in the ancient Vedic era, and its meaning and conceptual scope have evolved over the millennia. *Dharma* and related words are found in the oldest Vedic literature of Hinduism, including the Vedas, *Upanishads*, epics, and *Puranas* (to be discussed shortly).

Dharma is a concept of primary importance in Indian philosophy and religion, and it has multiple meanings in all indigenous Indian religions, including Hinduism and Buddhism. It describes the Hindu religion, its culture, duties, rights, laws, conduct, virtues, and the right way of living. It is immutable and eternal.[29] Nothing in Hinduism is higher than *dharma*; it is considered the truth. *Dharma* applies to human beings as well as inanimate objects, and the cosmos.[30]

Sacred Texts

Now that some basic concepts of Hinduism have been established, let's discuss some of its foundational religious writings, including (in order): the Vedas, *Upanishads*, *Mahabharata* and *Ramayana* epics, *Puranas*, and *Manusmriti*.[31] First, it should be noted that all of the sacred texts are perceived as religiously authoritative.[32] Hinduism started as an oral tradition where the material was memorized and passed along verbally from

28. Leidig, "Hindutva as a Variant of Right-wing Extremism," 217.
29. Cook, *Ancient Religions, Modern Politics*, 283.
30. Rosen, *Essential Hinduism*, 34-45.
31. Roy, *Hinduism and the Ethics of Warfare in South Asia*, 11.
32. Olivelle, *Upanishads*, lvii.

generation to generation.³³ When it was eventually put down in writing, the language normally used was Sanskrit, the language of the Aryans. Second, none of the sacred texts necessarily reflected reality or facts. The text were stories meant to illustrate philosophy and values.³⁴ Finally, authorship and dates were not important at that time, so no one really knows as much about the Far Eastern sacred texts as the Abrahamic sacred texts. According to Kaushik Roy, a professor at the Jadavpur University in Calcutta, India, "Dating and assigning authorship to various classical Hindu texts is almost impossible as the individual in society is unimportant."³⁵

Vedas

"Veda" is a Sanskrit word that means "knowledge." The Vedas are the foundation of Indian culture and the belief system of Hinduism. The Vedas are not the work of a single author, and many changes have been made to them over the millennia.³⁶ There are four main Vedas: Rig Veda, Sama Veda, Yajur Veda, and Atharva Veda; and all originated in written form between 1500-600 BCE.³⁷ According to Cook, "The foundation of Hinduism are the Vedas. The Vedas were manifestly the oldest textbook stratum of the Hindu tradition. The Rig Veda is the oldest text in current use in any of the world's religions. And, not just old, but eternal."³⁸ The first and most famous Veda is the Rig Veda.³⁹ It originated with the Aryans in the northern Punjab region of India between 1500-1200 BCE.⁴⁰ It is a collection of 1,028 hymns that identified three places gods lived; on earth, an intermediate region, and in the sky.⁴¹ The gods are associated with key aspects of nature, such as the sun, moon, storm, rivers, and fire.⁴² It also identifies the eternal cycle (i.e.,

33. Langley, *World Religions*, 19.
34. Roy, *Hinduism and the Ethics of Warfare in South Asia*, 8.
35. Roy, *Hinduism and the Ethics of Warfare in South Asia*, 7.
36. Olivelle, *Upanishads*, xxxii; https://arshabodha.org/teachings/short-articles/article-13/
37. Olivelle, *Upanishads*, xxx; Roy, *Hinduism and the Ethics of Warfare in South Asia*, 13.
38. Cook, *Ancient Religions, Modern Politics*, 400.
39. Doniger, *On Hinduism*, 6.
40. Cook, *Ancient Religions, Modern Politics*, 193.
41. Olivelle, *Upanishads*, xlvii.
42. Olivelle, *Upanishads*, xlvi.

life, death, and rebirth), from which there is normally no escape. However, the Rig Veda identified three ways to escape this endless cycle: 1) knowledge, 2) religious observance, and 3) religious devotion.[43] It also identified the related concept of karma.

Upanishads

Next are the *Upanishads*, a collection of philosophical dialogues and commentaries on the Vedas and other religious topics, which serve as the foundation of Hindu philosophical thought.[44] According to Patrick Olivelle, a professor of Sanskrit and Indian Religions in the Department of Asian Studies at the University of Texas, "The *Upanishads* played a critical role in the development of religious ideas in India."[45] The texts within the *Upanishads* were transmitted orally from generation to generation, perhaps for a thousand years, before being written down.[46] The word "*Upanishad*" has multiple meanings, including connections, equivalence, and secret.[47] The earliest copies of the *Upanishads* occurred between the 7th and 6th century BCE – before the emergence of Buddhism.[48] The authors of the *Upanishads* are anonymous with no evidence of authorship or dates.[49] There are many versions of the *Upanishads*, so there are many interpretations of it as well.[50] In fact, there are 108 known *Upanishads*, with only the first dozen or so considered the principal *Upanishads*.[51]

One of the key themes of the *Upanishads* is time. Everything is cyclic, starting with the universe and ending with each person. The universe grows, dies, and starts over. Like people, gods also die and are reborn. The only escape from this endless cycle of life, death, and rebirth is achieving *Moksha*.[52] Another related key aspect is the concept of merit. One earns

43. Langley, *World Religions*, 21.
44. Upanishadic philosophy is called *Vedanta* (Doniger, *On Hinduism*, 13).
45. Olivelle, *Upanishads*, xxiii.
46. Olivelle, *Upanishads*, xxxii; Roy, *Hinduism and the Ethics of Warfare in South Asia*, 7.
47. Olivelle, *Upanishads*, lii, liii.
48. Olivelle, *Upanishads*, xxxvi; Langley, *World Religions*, 19.
49. Olivelle, *Upanishads*, xxxiv.
50. Olivelle, *Upanishads*, lviii.
51. Phillips, *Yoga, Karma, and Rebirth*, 25–29.
52. Parrinder, *World Religions*, 209, 211.

merit during one's lifetime to improve one's status upon rebirth or to improve the status of a loved one who has already died.[53] One earns merit by doing good deeds, such as offering food to monks in the morning, building temples, or donating money to monasteries.

Today, Hindus worship hundreds of millions of gods. In the *Upanishads*, the many gods are reduced to one – *Brahman*.[54] In the beginning, there was only *Brahman*, who is the creator of *dharma* and who continues to be the all-pervading cosmic unity.[55] Anyone who attains the world of *Brahman* is no longer reborn.[56] All the gods in the Hindu pantheon of gods emanate from *Brahman*.

Gods

Practitioners of Hinduism generally acknowledge the existence of numerous deities and devote themselves to any number of them. However, some Hindus prefer to practice without any devotion to deities and thus recognize no deity or deities personally. In total, Hindus believe in as many as 330 million deities.[57] However, as mentioned earlier, Hindus are monotheistic at heart with *Brahman* as the supreme spirit and creator.[58] There are a multitude of gods that are considered manifestations of *Brahman*. While Hinduism accepts numerous divine beings, there are three major deities worth remembering along with *Brahman*: 1) *Vishnu*, the benevolent, supreme deity and preserver, with avatars (i.e., divine incarnations) including Lords *Krishna* and *Rama*; 2) *Shiva*, the god of destruction; and 3) *Shakti*,

---

53. Olivelle, *Upanishads*, 116.
54. Parrinder, *World Religions*, 16.
55. Olivelle, *Upanishads*, 16; Langley, *World Religions*, 20.
56. Olivelle, *Upanishads*, 176.

57. Roy, *Hinduism and the Ethics of Warfare in South Asia*, 10. One reason there may be over 300 million gods in India is probably because Hindus project human characteristics upon their gods, to include death. As such, for Hindus it is not realistic to believe one god could manage the personal lives of almost 1.4 billion people in India (2020 data). Given that the average family size in India is 4.6 people (https://www.prb.org/international/indicator/hh-size-av/map/country/) – compared to the average size in the US at 2.6 people), then that means there are around 300 million families in India, each praying to their own selected, personal god.

58. According to the *Vedanta* school of thought. Langley, *World Religions*, 21; Doniger, *On Hinduism*, 14.

the divine mother, also known as *Devi*.⁵⁹ Hinduism has a trinity of gods (analogous to the Trinity in Catholicism) that ascended into prominence during the Vedic period. This trinity is called the *Trimurti*, representing the cyclical nature of human as well as cosmic existence: *Brahma* the Creator, *Vishnu* the Preserver, and *Shiva* the Destroyer.⁶⁰

Hindus are advised early on to form lifelong attachments to one or more of the numerous deities of the pantheon of *Brahman* avatar gods. Many of the mythic narratives as well as common beliefs of Hindus emphasize that whenever the stability of the world is threatened, *Vishnu*, in his role as preserver of the universe, appears on earth in human form to redress the imbalance.⁶¹ In Hinduism, it is possible for human beings to become deified after their deaths, and many are revered as gods, including a number of sages. Both Jesus and Buddha, as well as divine beings in other religions, are considered avatars, with Buddha being considered as an avatar of *Vishnu*.⁶²

Bhakti is a Sanskrit word that refers to worship, devotion, and love for a specific god or many gods. It requires a relationship between the deity and the devotee.⁶³ Domestic *bhakti* shrines usually consist of butter lamps, colored lights, incense containers, and/or images of deities. These shrines can be in a corner of a room, the whole room, or a separate temple on one's property.⁶⁴

Epics

There are many oral epics in Hinduism, but only two are considered sacred—the *Mahabharata* and the *Ramayana*.⁶⁵ Epics are not recollections of historical events, but a mixture of legends, ballads, and myths.⁶⁶ Hindu

---

59. Doniger, *On Hinduism*, 14; Parrinder, *World Religions*, 192, 216, 222.

60. https://www.dailyartmagazine.com/gods-of-the-hindu-trinity-representation-in-art/#:~:text=The%20Hindu%20trinity%20comprises%20Brahma,preservation%2C%20destruction%20to%20subsequent%20regeneration.

61. Smith, *The World's Religions*, 36.

62. Cook, *Ancient Religions, Modern Politics*, 107; Langley, *World Religions*, 22.

63. DeNapoli, "Earning God Through the "One-Hundred Rupee Note" *Religions*, 408.

64. Roy, *Hinduism and the Ethics of Warfare in South Asia*, 182.

65. Roy, *Hinduism and the Ethics of Warfare in South Asia*, 11.

66. Roy, *Hinduism and the Ethics of Warfare in South Asia*, 18.

epics were eventually recorded in Sanskrit.[67] In both these epics, war was the last resort, and death in battle was considered glorious.[68] During the Gupta Empire (319-543 CE), which at its peak covered much of the Indian subcontinent, the sacred Hindu scripts of the *Mahabharata* and *Ramayana* were canonized.

Mahabharata Epic

The founding epic of Hinduism is the *Mahabharata* epic. It was written between the 5th and 3rd centuries BCE, and consists of 100,000 couplets, making it the longest poem in the world.[69] It contains the spiritual teachings of the Vedas. It is an epic poem about the dynastic succession struggle for the throne of Kuru Kingdom (located in northern India) between the Pandavas and their cousins, the Kaurava. The Pandavas, with the gods on their side, prevailed in this internecine conflict. The war lasted only eighteen days. It involved several ancient kingdoms allied with each side.[70]

Bhagavad Gita

The most famous part of the *Mahabharata* epic is the *Bhagavad Gita* ("Song of God"), written in the 2nd century BCE and declared a sacred text in Hinduism.[71] According to Cook, "The only text that was at all in competition with the Vedas was the celebrated *Bhagavad Gita*. In 1979, the International Hindu Conference proposed the *Bhagavad Gita* as the sacred book of the Hindus."[72]

The *Gita* consists of 700 verses in chapters 23-40 of the Book of *Bhishma*.[73] The story is about the Pandavan Prince Arjuna preparing to go into

---

67. Parrinder, *World Religions*, 215.

68. Roy, *Hinduism and the Ethics of Warfare in South Asia*, 31.

69. Roy, *Hinduism and the Ethics of Warfare in South Asia*, 14, Parrinder, *World Religions*, 214.

70. https://www.swarthmore.edu/friends-historical-library/why-religions-facilitate-war-and-how-religions-facilitate-peace

71. Cook, *Ancient Religions, Modern Politics*, 402, 418; Roy, *Hinduism and the Ethics of Warfare in South Asia*, 15.

72. Cook, *Ancient Religions, Modern Politics*, 402.

73. Roy, *Hinduism and the Ethics of Warfare in South Asia*, 15. The Book of Bhishma describes the first 10 days of the 18-day Kurukshetra War, and its consequences. It recites

the largest war in history up until that time. He is on his chariot and having second thoughts about going into battle for many reasons, beginning with the likely prospect of killing some of his relatives. Lord *Krishna*, one of the most important avatars of *Vishnu*, is Arjuna's guide and charioteer. The *Gita* is about the verbal interaction between Prince Arjuna and Lord *Krishna*. *Krishna* advises Arjuna to "fulfill his Kshatriya (warrior caste) and to uphold the *dharma*" by doing what he has trained and prepared to do – be a warrior and fight, no matter what the cost. Their dialogue covers a broad range of topics, including ethical dilemmas and philosophical issues beyond the impending battle.[74] Lord *Krishna* appears in the *Gita* in the form of every deity imaginable and emphasizes that everything in the universe comes from him, and therefore one part of existence killing another part is not truly any sort of loss or offense. This is the final message of the *Gita* which essentially does not condemn violence or warfare, but instead glorifies it.

Ramayana Epic

Turning to the *Ramayana* epic, it was written between the 7th and 4th centuries BCE, making it older than the *Mahabharata* epic.[75] As one of the longest ancient epic poems in world literature, it consists of nearly 24,000 verses, also written in Sanskrit. This epic is about the life of Lord Rama, an avatar of *Vishnu*, who was from the ancient Kingdom of Kosala. He was exiled to the Bharath forest for fourteen years with his wife, Sita, and brother, Lakshmana. The demon King Ravana of Lanka kidnaps Sita, resulting in a prolonged battle where good prevailed over evil. Rama eventually got his wife back. However, things did not go well for Rama in the end. He believed his wife bore illegitimate twin sons with King Ravana and he had her killed. Then, he drowned himself.[76]

---

the story of Bhishma, the commander in chief of the Kaurava armies, who was fatally injured.

74. Vyasa, translated by Telang, *The Bhagavad Gita*, 6.
75. Brockington, *The Sanskrit Epics*, 379.
76. Roy, *Hinduism and the Ethics of Warfare in South Asia*, 14.

Puranas

The word *Puranas* means "ancient or antiquities."[77] The *Puranas* were written in Sanskrit beginning around 250 CE and continued to be written for another millennium. It is a genre of Indian encyclopedic literature covering a wide range of legends, mythologies, and other traditional lore that are the common themes of Hinduism. The original *Puranas* comes from priestly roots, while the later versions come from warrior roots.

Manusmriti

Manusmriti (meaning the "Laws of Manu") is the most authoritative Hindu Law Book. It has served as a foundational work on Hindu law in ancient India for at least 1,500 years. It was codified around 1000 BCE. Until modern times, it was the standard reference for adjudicating civil and criminal cases used by the people who practiced Hinduism, to include justifying the caste system as the basis of an orderly society. Of the many law books in India, *Manusmriti* is the most popular and authoritative work.[78]

New Hinduism

Hindutva is the predominant form of Hindu nationalism in India today. It is often confused with "Hinduness." However, where Hinduism is compatible with liberalism and the protection of minority groups, *Hindutva* is opposed to both.[79] Robert Frykenberg, the former Chair of the Department of South Asian Studies at the University of Wisconsin, described *Hindutva* as:

> Extremely conservative, but also romantic, reactionary, and revivalist in character, [Hindutva is] defensive, chauvinistic, and xenophobic, especially in response to Western influences and negative attitudes of some foreign missionaries and officials, as well as Indian social reformers, toward ancient and hallowed Hindu cultures.[80]

---

77. Parrinder, *World Religions*, 215.
78. https://www.hinduwebsite.com/sacredscripts/hinduism/dharma/manusmriti.asp; https://www.bbc.com/news/world-asia-india-35650616
79. Vaishnav, "Religious Nationalism and India's Future," 15.
80. Sweetman and Malik, eds., *Hinduism in India*, 104.

The difference between *secular* and Hindu nationalism is that secular nationalism combines territory and culture, while Hindu nationalism combines territory and *religion*.[81] According to Ashutosh Varshney, a professor of political science at Brown University, "Secular and Hindu nationalism are ideological adversaries and have remained so for decades."[82] Hindu nationalism would be analogous to a theocratic form of government, such as that found in Iran.

Hindutva was created by Chandranath Basu in 1892 in his publication *Hindur Prakrita Itihas* and popularized by Vinayak Savarkar, a politician, in 1923 with his publication entitled "*Hindutva*." Basu and Savarkar wanted to demonstrate Hinduism's superiority over Christianity and Islam.[83] Savarkar was the president of the Hindu *Mahasabha*, a political party formed to protect Hindu rights, from 1937–1942. He was also a radical opponent of British rule in India.[84]

In *Hindutva*, Savarkar wrote that Hindus were those native people who lived in the Indian sub-continent and considered it their fatherland, motherland, and/or "Holyland."[85] This means that Muslims from Arabia and Christians from Europe and America cannot be (or even become) Hindus.[86] As well, Hindus shared common blood, meaning a Hindu's parents must also be Hindus.[87] Savarkar goes even further to claim Hindus are an ethnic group like Jews, hence, unlike Islam and Christianity.[88] Note that Savarkar was a self-described atheist, so his emphasis of *Hindutva* was Hindu ethnicity, culture, and geography. Savarkar had a maxim regarding *Hindutva*: "Hindu, Hindi, Hindustan"—based on religious identity, common language, and the entire geographic territory of India.[89]

Interestingly, Savarkar claimed that all religions within India source back to the ancient Hindu Vedas.[90] In Savarkar's view, Sikhs, Jains, and

81. Roy, *Hinduism and the Ethics of Warfare in South Asia*, 62.

82. Sweetman and Malik, eds., *Hinduism in India*, 69.

83. Gier, *The Origins of Religious Violence*, 29.

84. Rambachan, "The Coexistence of Violence and Nonviolence in Hinduism," 97.

85. Savarkar, *Essentials of Hindutva*, 71, 113.

86. Savarkar, *Essentials of Hindutva*, 113.

87. Savarkar, *Essentials of Hindutva*, 71, 110.

88. Savarkar, *Essentials of Hindutva*, 131.

89. Vaishnav, "Religious Nationalism and India's Future," https://www.hindustantimes.com/analysis/from-nation-state-to-state-nation/story-rm96nO2fLzyyGOSPOPIilN.html

90. Savarkar, *Essentials of Hindutva*, 92, 107.

other religions formed within India are all syncretic offshoots of Hinduism, while Islam and Christianity were alien religions in India.[91] The *Hindutva* movement also adopted and adapted elements from the Abrahamic religions, to include one almighty god (in this case, the Lord Rama), and one holy scripture (i.e., the *Upanishads*) to give Hinduism more credibility.[92] Note, however, that *Hindutva* is not able to provide a corresponding prophet such as Mohammad in Islam or Apostle Paul in Christianity because the Hindu culture has historically been focused on families, tribes, and groups – not individuals.

As such, *Hindutva* can be considered both a nationalist and a fundamentalist version of Hinduism (they are not the same). Cook does not accept that *Hindutva* is Hindu fundamentalism writing, "Some writers refer to Hindu nationalism as Hindu fundamentalism. But Hindu nationalists are religious nationalists, not religious fundamentalists."[93] However, most Indian scholars disagree claiming Hindu fundamentalism is in reality synonymous with *Hindutva*.[94]

Today, many Indians perceive *Hindutvans* as supporting the business community in India, who in turn support them.[95] Milan Vaishnav, the director of the South Asia Program at the Carnegie Endowment for International Peace, described *Hindutva's* threat to India's diversity stating that "Given India's stunning religious and cultural diversity, granting preferential treatment to Hinduism would have come at the cost of ensuring India's syncretic traditions."[96]

While Savarkar included Jains and Sikhs, and other native religions of India, a part of *Hindutva*, he made a point that this did *not* include Buddhists – even though Buddhism was created in India and is a direct offshoot of Hinduism.[97] He wrote, "We yield none of our love, admiration or respect to the Buddha, Dharma, or Sangha. . . . We do not believe the political virility, or the manly nobility began or ended or was a consequence

---

91. Rambachan, "The Coexistence of Violence and Nonviolence in Hinduism," 101.
92. Almond, Appleby, and Sivan, *Strong Religion*, 16.
93. Cook, *Ancient Religions, Modern Politics*, 309.
94. Anonymous, "Rise of Hindu Fundamentalism," https://www.lausanne.org/content/lga/2019-05/the-rise-of-hindu-fundamentalism
95. Anonymous, "Rise of Hindu Fundamentalism," https://www.lausanne.org/content/lga/2019-05/the-rise-of-hindu-fundamentalism.
96. Vaishnav, "Religious Nationalism and India's Future," 4.
97. Savarkar, *Essentials of Hindutva*, 126.

of Buddhism."[98] Savarkar went even further indicating that the pacifism of Buddhism caused Hindus to become weaker in the face of foreign threats. He wrote, "What was the use of a universal faith that instead of smoothening the ferociousness and brutal egoism of other nations only excited their lust by leaving India defenseless and unsuspecting?"[99] One significant difference between Hinduism and Buddhism is that Buddha rejected the caste system (to be discussed shortly) as promoting inequality. This anti-caste position did not align with Hindu culture and tradition. Savarkar concluded that Buddhism did not fit in Hindu culture, writing, "It was political and national necessity that was the cause of decline of Buddhism in India. Buddhism's center of gravity was nowhere."[100] He alleged that without Buddhism, Hindu military power would be more preeminent. He wrote, "Clear also was the fact that Buddhist logic had no argument that could efficiently meet this new and terrible dualism – this strange Bible of Fire and Steel. . . . The success of the renovated Hindu arms was undisputed and indisputable."[101]

The Great Hindu Council was created and *Hindutva* was first published in 1915.[102] *Hindutva* was then championed by the Hindu nationalist organization Rashtriya Swayamsevak Sangh (RSS) beginning in 1925. In 1951, the Bharatiya Janata Party (BJP) was founded, and took the *Hindutva* mantle from RSS. (The BJP is considered the *Brahmin* party.[103]) One goal of *Hindutva* is to restore *Akhand Bharat* ("Undivided India"). In 1937 at the Hindu *Mahasabha's* 19th annual session, Savarkar advocated a return to the original India, to include Pakistan, Afghanistan, Bangladesh, and even Nepal and Myanmar (formerly Burma).[104]

The BJP is one of two major political parties in India today, the other being the Indian National Congress party.[105] The BJP has ruled India since 2014 and became the largest political party in India in 2019. In the 2014 Indian general election, the BJP won 282 seats in parliament out of a possible

---

98. Savarkar, *Essentials of Hindutva*, 20.
99. Savarkar, *Essentials of Hindutva*, 25.
100. Savarkar, *Essentials of Hindutva*, 28.
101. Savarkar, *Essentials of Hindutva*, 21.
102. Almond, Appleby, Sivan, *Strong Religion*, 136.
103. Cook, *Ancient Religions, Modern Politics*, 88.
104. https://www.organiser.org/Encyc/2020/8/15/The-Idea-of-Akhand-Bharat.html
105. The Indian National Congress ruled India for much of the post-independence period and has promoted secular nationalism.

543 (31% of all votes cast). Narendra Modi, of the BJP, was sworn in as the 14th Prime Minister of India on May 26, 2014. The *Hindutva* political movement supports the right-wing extremist concept of a homogenized majority and the cultural hegemony of Hinduism over all other religions in India. As such, this has become a major source of conflict among religions in India today, especially with Islam. *Hindutva* finds more support in northern India than it does in the south.[106]

Branches

As with most religions, Hinduism developed into several branches. Most of the branches focus on one of the primary gods in the Hindu pantheon of gods. According to Roy, there are four main branches of Hinduism, including Brahmanism, Vedantism, Shakti, and Tantra. The Brahmanism branch focuses on the creator god, *Brahman*, and the relationship between one's eternal soul and the observed universe. The Vedantism branch focuses on the Vedas and the philosophies around knowledge and liberation. The Shakti branch focuses on the goddess *Devi* as the Supreme Brahman. Finally, the Tantra branch focuses on the liberation of energy and the expansion of consciousness.[107] Two more common branches of Hinduism include the Vaishnavas that focus on *Vishnu*, the Shaivites that focus on *Shiva*.

There is a relatively new type of Hinduism called *Brahmo Samaj* ("Men who worship Brahma") created by Ram Roy and Tagore in 1828 in Calcutta as a reaction to the prevailing Brahmanism. According to David Kopf, a professor of South Asian history at the University of Minnesota, it was one of the most influential religious movements in India in the 19th century.[108] It began the Bengal Renaissance, pioneering all religious, social, and educational advances of the Hindu community. From the *Brahmo Samaj* came Brahmoism, the most recent of legally- recognized religions in India and Bangladesh. Brahmoism is a monotheistic reformist movement of Hinduism, combining Sufism from Islam and Vedanta from Hinduism with Unitarianism from Christianity.[109]

---

106. Cook, *Ancient Religions, Modern Politics*, 73.
107. Roy, *Hinduism and the Ethics of Warfare in South Asia*, 10.
108. Kopf, *The Brahmo Samaj and the Shaping of the Modern Indian Mind*, 123.
109. Doniger, *On Hinduism*, 17.

Proselytizing

Hindus do not proselytize Hinduism primarily because the religion is inherently pluralistic and has the viewpoint that everyone must find their own way and do their own thing. Thus, to make others follow a particular way they have not found themselves might be a violation of their own karmic path. Hindus do not turn people away if they seek Hindu practices, because that, too, may be a part of that person's karmic path. The bottom line is Hindus do not actively seek to convert others—in most cases. As well, given the geography of South Asia, it would not be that easy to expand. Historically, Hinduism has remained pretty much within South Asia (much like Shinto has remained primarily in Japan).

Caste System

The Hindu caste system in India stratifies the entire population into different work groupings, arguably the world's "incarnation of hierarchism."[110] The Aryans developed the caste system during the ancient era likely to control the local population. The verses on Purusha in the *Rig Veda* are considered the origins of the system.[111] It eventually became a legal part of society when the aforementioned *Manusmriti* justified it as "the basis of order and regularity of society."[112] Notably, one is born into the caste of one's parents. As such, the caste classification is inherited and can last forever for one's family lineage.[113]

The caste system began in ancient India with just five castes to include the Brahmins,[114] the top caste consisting of Vedic intellectuals and spiritual leaders; Kshatriyas, the caste of warriors, royalty, and administrators; Vaishyas, the caste of farmers, merchants, and landowners; Shudras, the caste of servants, commoners, and unskilled laborers (i.e., blue collar workers); and Dalits (also known as Camars) who were the "untouchables" of

---

110. Cook, *Ancient Religions, Modern Politics*, 194.

111. Cook, *Ancient Religions, Modern Politics*, 412.

112. https://www.hinduwebsite.com/sacredscripts/hinduism/dharma/manusmriti.asp

113. Smith, *World's Religions*, 56.

114. Brahmins, for example, were considered gods on earth and advised the rulers in India.

HINDUISM

society because they usually worked in sanitation fields.[115] There was one other group known as Others that consisted primarily of foreigners and Muslims. Hindus believe that only members of the Brahmin caste can attain *Moshka*. There is no equality between castes, but it is more likely to exist within a caste.[116]

After India gained independence in 1947, India's new constitution banned discrimination based on caste. As such, caste designations were subsequently modified and renamed to "class" (in most cases). The Brahmin caste remains atop the "caste pyramid" consisting of less than 5 percent of the population. However, the Kshatriya caste is now referred to as the Forward Class, with around 20 percent of the population. The Vaishya and Shudra castes are now essentially the Other Backward Class (OBC), consisting of around 45 percent of the population. The Scheduled Caste and Scheduled Tribes (SC/ST) are referred to as the "Depressed classes," encompassing the former Dalit caste, with around 30 percent of the population.[117] (Reference chart below.)

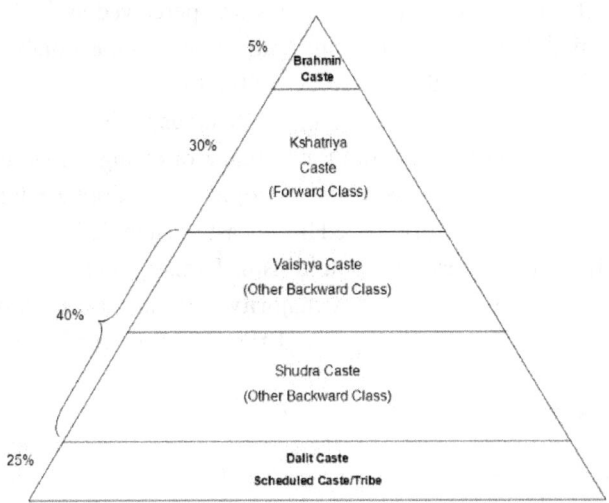

Indian Caste System[118]

115. Doniger, *On Hinduism*, 6; Smith, *World's Religions*, 56.

116. Smith, *World's Religions*, 57; https://www.bbc.com/news/world-asia-india-35650616

117. https://www.bbc.com/news/world-asia-india-35650616.

118. Author created.

Killing for Religion

The total number of castes has expanded over time. The main castes divided into around 3,000 castes today, and subsequently those divided into 25,000 sub-castes, again based on specific occupations.[119] One way to ensure people did not cross caste lines was by associating last names with each caste.[120] The caste members were generally forbidden to socialize in any way with someone not in their caste. To be clear, among other things, they were not allowed to share water, live together, accept food from, marry, date, work, or smoke with someone from another caste, especially from a higher one. For example, Brahmins would not accept free food or drink from a member of the Shudra caste. Castes were segregated in every way possible, from living in separate neighborhoods to socializing at different clubs. It is an extreme form of social segregation—with prejudice. When the British Raj assumed political and economic control of India in the mid-19th century, it embraced the caste system as one way to control the large population, much as the Aryans did in ancient times. For example, the British even integrated it into their periodic census of the population.[121]

The punishment for abusing the caste system has historically been severe. In the ancient era, crossing castes was perceived as "pollution that needed remedy," to include ex-communication.[122] One notable example was when Lord Rama killed a member of the lowly Shudra caste for a minor violation.[123] A few ways to change one's status within the caste system would be to become a monk, join the military, or change one's surname.[124] Another way to avoid the caste system would be to adopt a religion other than Hinduism. For centuries, the Hindu caste system led to tens of thousands of Indians converting to Buddhism, Jainism, Sikhism, or Islam.[125] Given that lower-caste Hindus (the majority of Indians today) tend to convert to either Islam or Buddhism, and that Muslims tend to have larger

---

119. Cook, *Ancient Religions, Modern Politics*, 58, 191–2.

120. Indian last names, particularly Hindu last names, are derived from religion, occupation, and region, much like other nationalities. But there is a fourth determinant in surnames: caste. The caste system, which determines a person's place in society, is now outlawed in India, but is still followed culturally. Singh, for example means "lion" and is usually associated with the warrior caste.

121. Cook, *Ancient Religions, Modern Politics*, 194.

122. Parrinder, *World Religions*, 215.

123. Juergensmeyer, Kitts, Jerryson, eds., *Violence and the World's Religious Traditions*, 26.

124. Roy, *Hinduism and the Ethics of Warfare in South Asia*, 3.

125. Gier, *The Origins of Religious Violence*, 7.

families than Hindus in general, one can see how followers of *Hindutva* perceive a growing threat from Muslims going forward.[126]

The caste system is often criticized for being unjust and repressive, trapping people into fixed social orders from which it is nearly impossible to escape. The caste system has been a public relations disaster for India as it has no counterpart in the modern world, and it counters the liberal philosophies of democracy, freedom, and equality. The caste system is exceptionally brutal to women, especially if they become widows. As well, the caste system results in a type of human bondage, much like slavery.[127] Cook declared the Hindu caste system as the "Achilles heel of Hindu identity."[128] He also observed that the caste system remains a central problem today of the Hindu nationalists.[129] As mentioned earlier, India adopted a new constitution in 1949 that made discrimination based on the caste system illegal. However, despite many attempts at all levels of government, the caste system continues to persist culturally in India today. Now that we have reviewed the basics of Hinduism, let us explore how it accommodates violence and conflict.

---

126. Cook, *Ancient Religions, Modern Politics*, 94.
127. Cook, *Ancient Religions, Modern Politics*, 194–5.
128. Cook, *Ancient Religions, Modern Politics*, 88.
129. Cook, *Ancient Religions, Modern Politics*, 415.

CHAPTER 4

Hinduism and Conflict

WE HAVE LEARNED THAT conflict is endemic within every religion, no matter how peaceful it purports to be. In this section, we will look at how conflict is facilitated within Hinduism. To begin, Michael Cook, a professor of Near Eastern Studies at Princeton University, observed that "Hinduism is a tradition that is comfortable with warfare,"[1] and that "War has an accredited place in the Hindu tradition."[2] As previously mentioned, some Asian religions adopted the Vedic concepts of *Himsa* and *Ahimsa*. *Himsa* is a Sanskrit term that means "to injure or harm." It describes causing physical or mental harm to others. *Ahimsa* has the opposite meaning – non-violence/no harm. *Ahimsa* became the highest virtue in the Vedic texts by around 500 BCE.[3] It was tied to the notion that any violence had adverse karmic consequences.[4] Putting these concepts into context, Anantanand Rambachan, a professor of religion, philosophy and Asian Studies at Saint Olaf College, observed that "Violence and non-violence in Hinduism has coexisted for centuries."[5]

There are a few key concepts regarding Hinduism and religious conflict. The first one is that, for Hindus, all religious conflict should be waged *justly*, with a moral purpose, peaceful aims, and employing lawful methods. Next, Kaushik Roy, a professor at the Jadavpur University in Calcutta, India, pointed out that "Offensive force in Hinduism is permissible only in

---

1. Cook, *Ancient Religions, Modern Politics*, 237.
2. Cook, *Ancient Religions, Modern Politics*, 235.
3. Tahtinen, "Non-violence as an Ethical Principle," 23–25.
4. Tahtinen, "Non-violence as an Ethical Principle," 23–25.
5. Rambachan, "The Coexistence of Violence and Nonviolence in Hinduism," 97.

reaction to a determinable wrong-doing."[6] Finally, force was to be used as a *last* resort. Stephen Jenkins, a professor of religious studies at Humboldt State University, explained why this was so, stating, "In Hindu sources, the common argument that war should be a last resort is grounded on the point that battle is *highly unreliable and unpredictable*."[7]

There are numerous examples of this throughout history. The one most Americans can relate to is the American Revolution, where George Washington led the Continental Army (a rag-tag militia of untrained and ill-equipped farmers) against the professional Imperial Army of Great Britain, the world power at the time. Despite all odds of success, Washington (with help from the French) won the critical Battle of Yorktown, and hence the war. This result was both highly unlikely and not expected, which is one reason why Hindus warn against rushing into war.

There are two sacred epics about war in Hinduism—*Mahabharata* and the *Ramayana*.[8] They discuss the numerous battles among the Aryan tribes in northern India.[9] As discussed within the *Bhagavad Gita*, the *Mahabharata* War was classified as a "*dharmayuddha*," a war fought in defense of justice and for the security and well-being of the community.[10] (Roy, however, found that both sides of the *Mahabharata* War were unclear about the rules for conducting "a just war."[11]) The *Mahabharata* War was an intra-Aryan, internecine war, while the war described in the *Ramayana* was against non-Aryans and non-humans (i.e., monkeys, bears, and demons).[12] It should be noted that these wars involved much killing, like many of the ancient European wars. Battles in ancient India were extremely bloody affairs.[13] As well, Roy reported that both of these sacred epics focused on heroic ideals.[14] He noted that there was a code of conduct for war in these two epics which included: 1) war must be declared; 2) combat must be ended at

---

6. Roy, *Hinduism and the Ethics of Warfare in South Asia*, 184.

7. Jerryson and Juergensmeyer, eds., *Buddhist Warfare*, 66.

8. Cook, *Ancient Religions, Modern Politics*, 241.

9. Cook, *Ancient Religions, Modern Politics*, 412; Roy, *Hinduism and the Ethics of Warfare in South Asia*, 21. Battle fought between groups of kings for territorial expansion. (Roy, *Hinduism and the Ethics of Warfare in South Asia*, 33)

10. Rambachan, "The Coexistence of Violence and Nonviolence in Hinduism," 97.

11. Roy, *Hinduism and the Ethics of Warfare in South Asia*, 27.

12. Roy, *Hinduism and the Ethics of Warfare in South Asia*, 34.

13. Roy, *Hinduism and the Ethics of Warfare in South Asia*, 19.

14. Roy, *Hinduism and the Ethics of Warfare in South Asia*, 19.

sunset, meaning no night fights; 3) prisoners should not be killed; and 4) spying was authorized. However, these rules were often broken during the Vedic epic battles.[15] Finally, while there were general guidelines based on just war among Hindus, there were almost no rules at all regarding conflict between Hindus and non-Hindus.[16]

In Hinduism, to fight is the duty of a warrior of the *Kshatriya* caste.[17] Even Brahmins, members of the religious (and highest) caste above the *Kshatriya* caste, served as generals in the 10th and 11th centuries.[18] In the Vedic era, death on the battlefield was considered "glorious."[19] In the *Mahabharata* War, one of *Vishnu's* avatars was Lord *Krishna*, who served as Prince *Arjuna's* charioteer. *Krishna* explained to *Arjuna*, a member of the *Kshatriyas* caste for rulers, nobles, and warriors, that he was expected to fight.[20] *Krishna* advocated for war and advised him that the violence was necessary.[21] (*Krishna* also believed that the ends justified any means.[22])

On the other hand, Mahatma Gandhi wanted Hinduism to be perceived as a peaceful religion—not one that accommodated conflict and warfare. Gandhi's primary focus was the principle of *ahimsa* which was the basis of his non-violent resistance against British colonial rule. He believed that the principle of non-violence was essential in providing the example of the moral superiority of non-violence over violence, even to the point of Indians being beaten and killed. Gandhi's non-violence principle became prominent in other civil rights struggles around the world (e.g., Reverend Dr. Martin Luther King, Jr., in his struggle for Black civil rights in the U.S.).

So, Gandhi decided to change the narrative of these two sacred war epics claiming that they were written as allegories of the conflict between truth and falsehood.[23] While that may be Gandhi's perception, it is not shared by most Hindus or religious scholars. As well, despite the clear

15. Roy, *Hinduism and the Ethics of Warfare in South Asia*, 35.

16. Cook, *Ancient Religions, Modern Politics*, 237.

17. Lehr, *Militant Buddhism*, 60.

18. Roy, *Hinduism and the Ethics of Warfare in South Asia*, 157.

19. Roy, *Hinduism and the Ethics of Warfare in South Asia*, 31.

20. The Kshatriyas, the group from which the kings and rulers were drawn, are the protectors of the community. They are the custodians of justice and the defenders of *dharma*, by the force of arms, if necessary. (Rambachan, "The Coexistence of Violence and Nonviolence in Hinduism," 97)

21. Jerryson and Juergensmeyer, *Buddhist Warfare*, 21, 25.

22. Roy, *Hinduism and the Ethics of Warfare in South Asia*, 36.

23. Jerryson and Juergensmeyer, *Buddhist Warfare*, 5.

connection of increased conflict when politics is mixed with religion, Gandhi believed that there was no politics devoid of religion.[24] (This position also goes contrary to Buddhism, which advocates for separation of religion and government.)

In general, the Aryans (the Indo-European people of northern India) engaged in conflict to acquire land, cattle, and even captives (to become slaves and servants).[25] Conflict throughout India in the recent past included infantry (including armed monks[26]), chariot warriors,[27] cavalry, and elephants.[28] In the Indus Valley of northern India, warfare was generally conducted between fortifications; hence, it was primarily defensive. Siege warfare was the strategy often employed, including setting the walls of enemy forts on fire.[29] To get an idea of the importance of warriors for Hindus, the *Rig Veda* says that a dead warrior has earned the same merit as the donor of a thousand cows.[30] As well, some Hindu castes believed that those who died in battle were received in heaven by beautiful maidens – analogous to the seventy-two black-eyed virgins believed to be awaiting Muslim martyrs.[31]

The most significant historic threat to Hinduism has been the encroachment of Islam as it was perceived as a violent, aggressive religion from a foreign land (i.e., the Middle East). Islam was being proselytized primarily by trade and force. Upon reaching India as early as the 6th century CE, Muslim forces usually defeated the Hindu armies.[32] By then, the pacificism of Buddhist influence was believed to have made Hinduism more vulnerable to the Muslim threat.[33] More recently, Gandhi, Savarkar, and other prominent Indians believed that Hindus in India were "deceived by European racial judgements" that they were "a weak and feminine people."[34] They blame Buddhism in part for their defeat by Muslim forces.

24. Roy, *Hinduism and the Ethics of Warfare in South Asia*, 224.
25. Roy, *Hinduism and the Ethics of Warfare in South Asia*, 21.
26. Roy, *Hinduism and the Ethics of Warfare in South Asia*, 172.
27. Roy, *Hinduism and the Ethics of Warfare in South Asia*, 20.
28. Roy, *Hinduism and the Ethics of Warfare in South Asia*, 19.
29. Roy, *Hinduism and the Ethics of Warfare in South Asia*, 25.
30. Roy, *Hinduism and the Ethics of Warfare in South Asia*, 31.
31. Roy, *Hinduism and the Ethics of Warfare in South Asia*, 182.
32. Gier, *The Origins of Religious Violence*, 5.
33. Gier, *The Origins of Religious Violence*, 28.
34. Gier, *The Origins of Religious Violence*, 34.

Muslims ruled over the Indian subcontinent for over six centuries starting with the Delhi Sultanate and Mamluk Dynasty, both beginning in 1206 CE. In 1526 CE, Babur, an Uzbek warrior chieftain descendant from Genghis Kahn, conquered the entire Indian sub-continent, and established an early modern empire known as the Mughal Empire lasting for more than two centuries.[35] (He received support and aid from the neighboring Safavid and Ottoman Muslim empires.) Muslim rule over India ended when the British East India Company took over in the mid-18th century and forced them out.

In India, the British leadership played the Hindus and Muslims off against each other for close to ninety years based on its "divide and rule" policy. For example, this policy included the creation of separate electorates for Muslims and Hindus. However, many Hindus still remember the oppressive Muslim rule in India, and they still harbor a desire for revenge.[36]

Hinduism and Conflict Today

Religious intolerance is at an all-time high in India today, especially if one is a Muslim or a Christian. A 2015 PEW Research Center analysis of 198 countries in the world ranked India as the fourth worst for religious intolerance.[37] The main reason for this low ranking is the rise of *Hindutva* in India over the past few decades. It has emerged as the nationalist and fundamentalist version of Hinduism.[38] Gabriel Almond, a professor of political science for multiple universities to include Yale, Princeton, and Stanford, observed that "Hindu fundamentalism clearly seeks to conquer India and replace its secular constitution with something based on *Hindutva*."[39] *Hindutva* claims to promote Hindu values, way of life, history, ancestry, and culture, while representing all citizens who accept India as their holy land. *Hindutva* is the religious belief of the Rashtriya Swayamsevak Sangh (RSS), a volunteer paramilitary organization founded in 1925. Many consider the RSS to be a violent right-wing organization that promotes *Hindutva* and

---

35. Baumer, *The History of Central Asia*, 47.

36. Gort, Jackson, and Vroom, eds., *Religion, Conflict and Reconciliation*, 55; Almond, Appleby, Sivan, *Strong Religion*, 42.

37. https://www.pewforum.org/2017/04/11/global-restrictions-on-religion-rise-modestly-in-2015-reversing-downward-trend/

38. Eviane Leidig, "Hindutva as a variant of right-wing extremism," 223.

39. Almond, Appleby, Sivan, *Strong Religion*, 176.

supports the Bharatiya Janata Party (India's People Party—BJP).[40] The BJP is one of two major political parties in India (the other being the Indian National Congress). The BJP is a conservative political party, and it follows *Hindutva* religious beliefs about who is a Hindu and the primacy of Hinduism in India. As of 2019, the BJP had approximately 180 million members making it the country's largest political party and the world's largest political party in terms of membership.

The BJP first came to power briefly in 1996 as part of a coalition government. It returned to power in a coalition of political parties from 1998–1999. It returned in another coalition from 1999 to 2004. Finally, in 2014, the BJP won an absolute parliamentary majority and did so again in the 2019 general election.

Hindutva has much in common with Italian Fascism and German Nazism of the early 20th century. Eviane Leidig, a sociology researcher at the University of Oslo, noted *Hindutva's* early links with Italian Fascism and German Nazism. The commonality included being a Hindu was a matter of race and blood, not only a matter of culture. This idea was similar to the racial myths elaborated by both Germany and Italy.[41] Both the Germans and Italians had mutually beneficial relationships with *Hindutva* leadership.[42] Nazi propagandists and German businesses funded *Hindutva* publications in German newspapers, while at the same time *Hindutva* writers supported Germany's Jewish policy (i.e., the Holocaust) and advocated for National Socialism for India and a "Hindu Fuehrer" in local Indian newspapers.[43]

In 2014, Narendra Modi, leader of the BJP and lifelong supporter of the RSS, the primary Hindutvan organization, campaigned and was elected to become prime minister. One of the political platforms that he ran on was a recurring *Hindutva* theme of the Muslim threat to Hindus. He portrayed Muslims as the internal foreign invader and British colonialism as the external foreign invader.[44] Modi sees the Muslim threat from a few angles. First, Muslims are more united in India than Hindus. Next, Muslims tend to have larger families than Hindus. Finally, lower-caste Hindus are converting in droves to Islam to escape the caste system.[45] Next, Modi linked *Hindutva*

---

40. Leidig, "Hindutva as a Variant of Right-wing Extremism," 215.
41. Leidig, "Hindutva as a Variant of Right-wing Extremism," 215, 220.
42. Leidig, "Hindutva as a Variant of Right-wing Extremism," 221.
43. Leidig, "Hindutva as a Variant of Right-wing Extremism," 222.
44. Leidig, "Hindutva as a Variant of Right-wing Extremism," 219.
45. Cook, *Ancient Religions, Modern Politics*, 94.

to citizenship in India.⁴⁶ After four years, Modi ran for re-election and was even more successful than in 2014. At this point, one could make the case that *Hindutva* has become widely supported in India.⁴⁷

One of *Hindutva's* political platforms is to restore *Akhand Bharat* (Undivided India). To further that goal, Prime Minister Modi asked the Parliament to revoke Article 370 of the Indian Constitution, which ended the special regional status for the Jammu and Kashmir regions in the far north. This revocation occurred in August 2019, and it also permanently annexed these areas into India.⁴⁸ Modi imposed an indefinite lockdown on the area because of the unrest this action caused. As well, Modi's Parliament passed the Citizen's Amendment Bill in December 2019 which established a religious test for migrants who wanted to become citizens. The lockdown in Kashmir and the new citizenship law were perceived as discriminatory toward Muslims, thereby causing nationwide protests.

Two significant examples of the conflict supported by *Hindutva* against Muslims occurred in opposite locations in India. First, in the 16th century, a Mughal general, Mir Baqi, built a mosque, known as the *Babri Masjid*, on a site identified as the birthplace of the Hindu Lord Rama in the city of Ayodhya, in Uttar Pradesh (an eastern state in India). It had been the subject of a lengthy socio-political dispute and was targeted after a political rally of 150,000 volunteers organized by the BJP in December 1992. However, the rally turned violent, and the mob quickly overwhelmed security forces and tore down the mosque. This action led to extensive intercommunal rioting between Hindus and Muslims in not only India, but in Pakistan and Bangladesh as well, causing the death of at least two thousand people.⁴⁹

The second incident took place in February 2002, a decade after the *Babri Masjid* attack. A train returning from a pilgrimage with fifty-nine Muslims on it was intentionally set on fire at a train station in the western state of Gujurat, India, burning all of the Muslims to death. That was followed by a pogrom against Muslims throughout the state for weeks, with the blessing of state officials and law enforcement.⁵⁰ Close to two thousand more people were killed (and many more than that were injured),

---

46. Leidig, "Hindutva as a Variant of Right-wing Extremism," 219.
47. Leidig, "Hindutva as a Variant of Right-wing Extremism," 227.
48. Leidig, "Hindutva as a Variant of Right-wing Extremism," 227.
49. Gort, Jackson, and Vroom, eds., *Religion, Conflict and Reconciliation*, 51.
50. Gier, *The Origins of Religious Violence*, 40.

with Muslims being killed three times more than Hindus. International agencies, such as Human Rights Watch and Amnesty International, documented human rights violations, including rape and torture.[51]

While there has been conflict throughout India, primarily between Hindus and Muslims, Paul Brass, a professor of political science and international relations at the University of Washington, determined there were other factors involved than just religious differences. He argued that the historical sources of conflict also had to do with political and economic power.[52] He also noted that the recent periodic religious riots around India were usually related to upcoming political elections.[53] Jerald Gort, a professor of theology at the Free University in Amsterdam, concurred writing, "Even today, political leaders in India play an important role in the escalation of religious conflicts, only for electoral gain."[54] In any case, there are more Muslims in India (around 195 million in 2020) than in all but two countries in the world today – Indonesia (229 million) and Pakistan (200 million).[55] As such, the intercommunal religious conflict is likely to continue in India for the foreseeable future.

While Savarkar belittled Buddhism as a "pacifist" religion that weakened Hinduism, in fact, Buddhism accommodates and facilitates conflict and violence far more than Hinduism has. But first, we must review the basics of Buddhism in the next chapter.

---

51. Leidig, "Hindutva as a Variant of Right-wing Extremism," 225.
52. Brass, *The Production of Hindu-Muslim Violence in Contemporary India*, 26–7.
53. Brass, *The Production of Hindu-Muslim Violence in Contemporary India*, 34.
54. Gort, Jackson, and Vroom, eds., *Religion, Conflict and Reconciliation*, 53.
55. https://worldpopulationreview.com/country-rankings/muslim-population-by-country

CHAPTER 5

Buddhism

UNLIKE HINDUISM, WHICH ENCOMPASSES the traditional beliefs of the people in the South Asian subcontinent, Buddhism spread throughout South Asia, then into Southeast and East Asia. Huston Smith, a professor at multiple universities (the last being the University of California at Berkeley) and an author of thirteen books on religion and philosophy, noted that "Unlike Hinduism, which emerged by slow, largely imperceptible spiritual accretion, the religion of the Buddha appeared overnight, fully formed. In large measure it was a religion against Hindu perversions—an Indian *Protestantism*."[1] As one of only three global religions, Buddhism has the fourth largest number of adherents in the world today, with over 520 million followers.[2] Buddhism encompasses a variety of beliefs, traditions, and spiritual practices that originated in the Ganges Plain in northern ancient India sometime between the 6th and 4th centuries BCE, making it around 2,500 years old. As such, it is *not* older than Hinduism.[3] Many Buddhists believe Buddhism is superior to other religions because it is based on wisdom and understanding and not on superstition and the supernatural.[4] As an Indian religion, Buddhism was founded on the teachings of a mendicant commonly referred to as the Buddha ("the Awakened One"), which is a title and not a formal name.

1. Smith, *The World's Religions*, 92.
2. The other two global religions (both larger than Buddhism) are Christianity and Islam.
3. Bechert and Gombrich, eds., *The World of Buddhism*, 9.
4. Bechert and Gombrich, eds., *The World of Buddhism*, 278.

Gautama

Let us first discuss who the Buddha was to put this religion into context. His name was Siddhartha Gautama of the Shakya clan.[5] Historically, he was born in 596 BCE in Lumbini and grew up in the Shakya capital of Kapilavastu (in the Ganges Plain along the current India-Nepal border). His parents were King Suddhodana and Queen Maha Maya.[6] They were Hindus and belonged to the Kshatriya (royal/warrior) caste of society, the superior caste at the time.[7] As the oldest son, Gautama was being groomed to become king. At sixteen years old, he married a cousin, and they eventually had a son named Raula.[8]

Early on, King Suddhodana sought the predictions of eight Hindu Brahmins concerning Gautama's future. Most indicated he would become a religious ascetic (i.e., someone who practices severe self-discipline and abstinence). To combat this prophecy, the King restricted Prince Gautama to the palace grounds to protect him and to lavish him with luxuries—to include three palaces and 40,000 showgirls.[9] However, at the age of twenty-nine, Gautama finally left the palace to see what life was like on the outside. On his first excursion, he ran into some elderly people, which surprised him as he had not seen any before. On his second journey, he ran into sick and diseased people, which distressed him. On his third trip, he found a dead body, which made him contemplate the meaning of life and death. On his final excursion, Prince Gautama ran into an ascetic who had devoted himself to discover the cause of human suffering. Gautama decided that this is what he wanted to do with his life, and subsequently left his wife, son, the palaces, and all his worldly things to begin a quest to discover and end human suffering as an ascetic (as was predicted).[10]

In his quest, Gautama visited many spiritual experts to gain insight on how to end suffering. He was not satisfied with their teachings and began practicing severe asceticism by withdrawing from the world and practicing abstinence from everything except what was needed to keep alive. This effort failed to provide the insight he was looking for. So, after six years of

---

5. Smith, *The World's Religions*, 83.
6. Smith, *The World's Religions*, 83. More of a feudal lord than a king.
7. Jerryson, *Buddhist Fury*, 10, 158; Lehr, *Militant Buddhism*, 67.
8. Gier, *The Origins of Religious Violence*, 110.
9. Smith, *The World's Religions*, 84.
10. Smith, *The World's Religions*, 84.

wandering, he focused on meditating to find a solution. While meditating for forty-nine straight days under a tree in the town of Bodh Gaya, Gautama attained "awakening."[11] He self-declared, "By instructing myself, I have attained Enlightenment. I am the teacher of all gods and men, omniscient and endowed with powers. *I have vanquished Mara, I am the conqueror.*"[12] (Mara is a Sanskrit word meaning death or the personification thereof.)[13] As a fully enlightened "Buddha," he knew how people could end their ceaseless suffering. Interestingly, there is no explanation in the sacred texts as to exactly how Gautama achieved his Buddhahood enlightenment under a bodhi tree while meditating.[14] Finally, each Buddha over eternity has a unique name. Gautama was known as the Shakyamuni Buddha.[15]

Gautama spent the next forty-five years of his life (from 561-516 BCE) teaching his self-revealed beliefs, known as *dharma*.[16] His teachings included challenging each individual to do their own spiritual seeking ("Lamps unto yourselves"), distaining any religious rituals or traditions, and, renouncing the world (free from social and family ties and the need to earn a living) to seek a life of meditation.[17] His daily routine included public preaching and private counseling.[18]

Gautama attracted many followers who became the first monastic order (called the *Sangha*). He acquired a reputation for being quite the diplomat with his efforts to avoid war, convincing kings to negotiate rather than resort to armed aggression.[19] He eventually died in Kushingar, India, at the age of eighty, from dysentery after eating a meal of dried boar's flesh at a blacksmith's home.[20] He died as a mortal human being and not as a deity.

11. Smith, *The World's Religions*, 86.

12. Bechert and Gombrich, eds., *The World of Buddhism*, 43.

13. Fronsdal, *The Dhammapada*, xxvi.

14. The *Ariyaparitesanasutta* is completely silent on how the Buddha reached Nirvana . . . (Pyysiainen, "Buddhism, Religion, and the Concept of God," 152)

15. Shinozaki, Ziporyn, Earhart, translators, *The Threefold Lotus Sutra*, xv.

16. Berchert and Gombrich, eds., *The World of Buddhism*, 16, 42; Smith, *The World's Religions*, 87, 112.

17. Smith, *The World's Religions*, 9, 94-6.

18. Smith, *The World's Religions*, 87.

19. https://www.worldtribune.org/2016/12/sgi-buddhism-stand-issues-war-peace/

20. Smith, *The World's Religions*, 87. It is interesting to note that Gautama died from eating boar (an uncastrated male pig). The Prophet Mohammad revealed in four places in the Qur'an that Muslims were forbidden from eating pork because pigs consume filth hence are unclean and unsafe to eat.

However, his followers in Sri Lanka believe he is present today through his relics (to include body parts) stored in stupas (mound-like temples used for meditation).[21] Unlike Jesus Christ (son of a carpenter) and Prophet Mohammad (a merchant), Gautama died as a prince and politician.[22] Gautama is reported never to have answered the question of where he would be after his death.[23]

Syncretism

Before going any further, let us consider the relationship between Buddhism and Hinduism at that time. Hinduism had been around for quite a while before Gautama arrived. As a Hindu, he most likely learned about the Hindu religion from Brahmins. As such, he likely adopted many of his beliefs from Hinduism. This comingling of religious beliefs is known as *syncretism*, combining different beliefs and schools of thought, especially regarding religion. Moreover, it goes both ways. Once Buddhism became an established religion, critical Hindu thinkers were, in turn, influenced by Buddhist ideas. In fact, Hinduism's religious offshoots received a term – *Sramana* tradition, which includes Buddhism, Jainism, Sikhism, among others. *Sramana* tradition refers to several non-Hindu movements that parallel the Vedic religion (the foundation of Hinduism). For example, these religions tend to be autonomous with no governing body. As well, there are references to the Hindu supreme god, Brahman, found in the oldest Buddhist texts to explain Buddhist ideas. According to Smith,

> Buddhism was not so much defeated by Hinduism as accommodated within it. Up to around the year 1000 CE, Buddhism persisted in India as a distinct religion. The fact is that in the course of its 1,500 years in India, Buddhism's differences with Hinduism softened . . . Buddhist teachings came to sound increasingly like Hindu ones as Buddhism opened into the Mahayana, until in the end, Buddhism sank back into the source from which it had sprung.[24]

As such, one could characterize Buddhism as the *export version* of Hinduism. In China, it was Daoism that facilitated Buddhism within the

21. Pyysiainen, "Buddhism, Religion, and the Concept of God," 150, 160.
22. Jerryson, *Buddhist Fury,* 59.
23. Pyysianen, "Buddhism, Religion, and the Concept of God," 160.
24. Smith, *The World's Religions,* 148.

country. Where Daoists expanded their ideas about the cosmos and ways to structure their monastic orders from Buddhism, Buddhists used ideas from Daoism and the Chinese language to make Buddhism easier to teach and propagate in China.[25]

One aspect about religions is their extensive use of numbering to assist followers in remembering key concepts. This numerology may exist to give the concepts more legitimacy; however, it also makes it easier for people to memorize. The first key concept in Buddhism is the Three Jewels.

Three Jewels

A Buddhist from any of the various traditions and schools of Buddhism takes refuge and seeks salvation from what is referred to as the "Three Jewels": 1) Buddha, 2) *Dharma*, and 3) *Sangha*.[26] Etienne Lamotte, a Belgian priest and professor who taught at Catholic University in Louvain, offered an excellent way to view the relationship between these three jewels. The Buddha is perceived as the physician, the *dharma* as the remedy, and, the *Sangha* as the nurse.[27] As we discussed the Buddha at the beginning of this section (see Gautama), let us now discuss the *dharma* and the *Sangha*.

Dharma

In Hinduism, *dharma* is a Vedic word that reflects religious living in India. It applies to people, things, and the universe. It designates the way things are and must be – these have to coincide.[28] As the concept of *dharma* evolved among the religions in India, Gautama likely embraced it from Hinduism and modified it to accommodate his beliefs. As such, *dharma* in Buddhism refers to the body of Buddha's teaching, particularly the Four Noble Truths and the Noble Eightfold Path (to be discussed shortly).[29] This is in contrast to the *dharma* of Hinduism, which reflects the Indian culture, duties, rights, laws, conduct, virtues, and the right way of living.[30] The Buddhist *dharma*

---

25. https://asiasociety.org/buddhism-china
26. Bechert and Gombrich, eds., *The World of Buddhism*, 13.
27. Bechert and Gombrich, eds., *The World of Buddhism*, 41.
28. Bechert and Gombrich, eds., *The World of Buddhism*, 12.
29. Ford, *Cold War Monks*, 3.
30. Cook, *Ancient Religions, Modern Politics*, 283.

focuses on Buddhist sacred texts and not on the teachings of Hindu sacred texts, such as the Vedas and *Upanishads*, the caste system, or various Hindu schools of thought.

Sangha

Sangha is a Sanskrit word meaning "association" or "community." More commonly, *Sangha* refers to people who have left home voluntarily to become wandering ascetics. The term has long been used by various Indian religions, including Buddhism, Jainism, and Sikhism. As the third "jewel" in Buddhism, *Sangha* refers to the monastic community of ordained monks or nuns who have accepted the Buddhist *dharma* and chosen to follow the Buddha's ascetic way of life.[31]

Gautama originally established the *Sangha* in the fifth century BCE to provide a means for those who wished to practice Buddhism full-time, free from daily life's responsibilities. The *Sangha* has historically assumed responsibility for maintaining the integrity of the Buddhist doctrine as well as the translation and the teaching of Buddhism. The bottom line is that with no *Sangha*, there would be no Buddhism.[32]

Each Buddhist monastery has its own individual *Sangha*. As such, not all *Sanghas* are the same. First, there are separate male and female *Sanghas*, with the female *Sanghas* being subordinate.[33] *Sanghas* range from hardliner and extremist to progressive and moderate, both religiously and politically.[34] According to Michael Carrithers, a professor of anthropology at Durham University, "Today, the *Sangha* have split along party lines."[35] *Sanghas* tend to consist of the elites of society, meaning no downtrodden people, soldiers, or slaves are accepted.[36] However, *Sanghas* did employ slaves as servants within their monasteries.[37]

---

31. Nuns are formally subordinate to monks in the Sangha. In certain Buddhist movements and circles, the extended Sangha includes all dedicated Buddhist practitioners (rather than just monks/nuns). (Bechert and Gombrich, eds., *The World of Buddhism*, 13)

32. Bechert and Gombrich, eds., *The World of Buddhism*, 9.

33. Victoria, *Zen at War*, 196.

34. Lehr, *Militant Buddhism*, 4.

35. Bechert and Gombrich, eds., *The World of Buddhism*, 146.

36. Lehr, *Militant Buddhism*, 102.

37. Bechert and Gombrich, eds., *The World of Buddhism*, 138.

KILLING FOR RELIGION

History has shown the symbiotic relationship between *Sanghas* and royalty or government in every country or realm that adopted Buddhism as its official religion. *Sanghas* provide kings and governments legitimacy in the eyes of the people. In return, the king or government supports the *Sanghas*. This relationship included involvement in state affairs by members of the *Sangha* and involvement by the ruler in *Sangha* affairs, both for political reasons.[38] Often, the monarch would feel the need to "purify" the *Sangha*. For example, Emperor Ashoka disrobed (i.e., removed) the lazy, corrupted, and "gourmet" monks.[39]

Monks

To begin, the word "monk" comes from the Greek word "monos," which means *alone*. The belief in "I" or "me" is incompatible with Buddhism.[40] In order to attain *Nirvana*, according to the *Theravada* Buddhist tradition, one must become a monk or a nun. According to Richard Gombrich, a professor of religion at Oxford University and president of the Oxford Centre for Buddhist Studies, "To become a monk should be the final goal of every Buddhist since only through monastic life can one hope to achieve salvation."[41] There are four roles monks can assume: 1) ceremonial specialists, 2) property manager, 3) politician, or 4) forest dweller.[42] These roles will be discussed during this chapter.

Monks and nuns generally own few possessions due to their vows as renunciates, to include three robes, an alms bowl, a cloth belt, a needle and thread, a razor for shaving the head and eyebrows (at least once a month), and a water filter (in practice, they can have a few additional personal possessions, such as photographs). Monks renounce all other possessions. They cannot practice a career, nor can they receive, specifically, gold or silver (i.e., money).[43] Monks live on food collected during morning alms. They must accept whatever is offered to them.[44] Gombrich noted that "The more austere the way of life of a monk or group of monks, the more lay

38. Lehr, *Militant Buddhism*, 103-4, 106.
39. Bechert and Gombrich, eds., *The World of Buddhism*, 142.
40. Smith, *The World's Religions*, 49.
41. Bechert and Gombrich, eds., *The World of Buddhism*, 35.
42. Bechert and Gombrich, eds., *The World of Buddhism*, 134.
43. Smith, *The World's Religions*, 162–3.
44. Lehr, *Militant Buddhism*, 89.

veneration and charity they attract; the charity in turn usually mitigates their austerity."[45]

In many monasteries, eating food at any other time than in the morning or midday can result in punishment. While eating something that has been killed (e.g., pork from a pig) is frowned upon, most monks choose not to be vegetarians—so eating meat is not uncommon.[46] Alcohol is forbidden. Monks have no fixed residence other than their monastery. Monks are forbidden from being alone with any woman. In monasteries, chores are assigned to every monk. Hierarchy among monks is determined by merit and ordination seniority at the monastery.[47] At some monasteries, particularly Zen monasteries, senior monks act like drill sergeants. Discipline, obedience, conformity, and physical and mental endurance are features of monastic life.[48] In some Southeast Asian countries, afternoons at monasteries are used for military training against a perceived Muslim threat. Often soldiers are sent to monasteries to make merit (to be discussed).[49]

To formally become a monk and join a *Sangha*, one must request ordination to be conferred by at least ten monks and announce three times the intent to take refuge in the aforementioned Three Jewels. To be ordained, candidates must prove they are at least twenty years old, in good health, have no debt, not wanted for any crimes, and have the consent of relatives or wives.[50] The ordination ceremony includes an oral examination of selected scriptures. When initiates declare "refuge," they accept the Buddha, the *dharma*, and the *Sangha*. Then, they are shaven, dressed, and given a begging bowl and water pot.[51] Once these steps are accomplished, the senior monk declares "Come monk" to complete the process.[52]

The number one duty of a monk is to meditate about the *dharma*. The second duty is to study Buddhist scripture.[53] The greatest service a

---

45. Bechert and Gombrich, eds., *The World of Buddhism*, 81.

46. Baird, "Lao Buddhist Monks Involvement in Political and Military Resistance to the Lao People's Democratic Republic Government since 1975," 656.

47. Bechert and Gombrich, eds., *The World of Buddhism*, 56–58; Smith, *The World's Religions*, 58.

48. Victoria, *Zen at War*, 184.

49. Jerryson, *Buddhist Fury*, 67, 105.

50. Smith, *The World's Religions*, 164.

51. Smith, *The World's Religions*, 81.

52. Bechert and Gombrich, eds., *The World of Buddhism*, 55.

53. Lehr, *Militant Buddhism*, 83, 86.

monk can provide laypeople is to preach the words of the Buddha.[54] Another typical service that all monks provide is officiating at funerals because death is at the center of Buddhist spiritual awareness.[55] Buddhist monks are not priests and, as such, have no spiritual authority over laypeople (i.e., monks cannot absolve laypeople of their sins).[56] Monks also differ from priests in that they do not have frequent contact with laypeople but tend towards seclusion.[57] On the other hand, monks participate in confessing their own sins at least twice a month within their monastery.[58] As well, all monks are equal with equal rights.[59] However, when it comes to respect, monks receive more respect than teachers, who in turn receive more respect than parents.[60] Note that Buddhist obligations taken by a monk do not automatically entail a lifelong commitment. Monks are not forbidden from leaving the *Sangha* or monastery and can return to lay (everyday) life for any reason whenever they may decide to do so. Moreover, as long as monks live a good life as laypersons, they can be ordained again and return to the *Sangha* and monastery at any time.[61]

Throughout Buddhist history, meditation has been primarily practiced within monasteries. Buddhist devotion is usually focused on some object, image, or location that is seen as holy. Examples of objects of devotion include paintings or statues of Buddha, stupas, and bodhi trees. In Buddhism, there is a close relationship between the triad of the laypeople, government, and Buddhism.[62] According to the Buddha, politics is part of life, just as religion is. As such, the two cannot be separated.[63] In general, monks see themselves as social activists and political entrepreneurs to guide their parishioners politically.[64] Those monks that are *actively* in-

---

54. Smith, *The World's Religions*, 30.
55. Bechert and Gombrich, eds., *The World of Buddhism*, 14.
56. Lehr, *Militant Buddhism*, 85.
57. Smith, *The World's Religions*, 13.
58. https://fpmt.org/mandala/archives/older/mandala-issues-for-1996/september/the-benefits-of-being-monks-and-nuns/
59. Gier, *The Origins of Religious Violence*, 110.
60. Jerryson, *Buddhist Fury*, 55.
61. Bechert and Gombrich, eds., *The World of Buddhism*, 55; Lehr, *Militant Buddhism*, 94–5.
62. Lehr, *Militant Buddhism*, 54.
63. Lehr, *Militant Buddhism*, 131.
64. Lehr, *Militant Buddhism*, 111; Bechert and Gombrich, eds., *The World of Buddhism*, 145.

volved in politics are perceived as "dark monks" because politics is contrary to their vow of renunciation.[65] Although these monks are highly articulate, and can achieve influence and notoriety, they are a very small minority, even in the cities.[66]

Monasteries

Buddhist institutions, such as the *Sangha*, are centered around monasteries and temples. Again, according to *Theravada* Buddhist tradition, only through monastic life can a monk or nun hope to achieve salvation.[67] Monasteries offer the safest and most suitable environment for monks and nuns seeking enlightenment and *Nirvana* (to be discussed soon) due to the challenges and temptations of everyday life. Michael Jerryson, professor of religious studies at Youngstown University, noted that "Buddhist monasticism entails the separation of one's self from life's vulgarities."[68] Monastic affairs are managed by a general meeting of all monks or nuns. All decisions require unanimous consent of the assembled three times. A committee of elders is charged with resolving disputed issues.[69]

Next, as there is no caste system in Buddhism, positions at any monastery are based on seniority and merit.[70] According to Gombrich, "The position of the monastic order in Buddhism is even more dominant than the church of Christianity."[71] Brian Victoria, a Zen Buddhist priest, described the seniority system at monasteries as follows,

> Once permitted to enter the monastery, monks find that everyone is their superior – even if it arrived only hours before. Senior monks wore finer and more colorful robes and lived in more spacious quarters. The senior monks can even leave the monastery for short periods of time, eat meat, drink alcohol, and keep petty money and gifts made to the monastery.[72]

65. Lehr, *Militant Buddhism*, 6, 257; Generally, renunciation is the giving up of actions and desires that are unwholesome, such as lust for sensuality and worldly things.
66. Lehr, *Militant Buddhism*, 256.
67. Bechert and Gombrich, eds., *The World of Buddhism*, 35.
68. Jerryson, *Buddhist Fury*, 4.
69. Victoria, *Zen at War*, 195.
70. Gier, *The Origins of Religious Violence*, 111.
71. Bechert and Gombrich, eds., *The World of Buddhism*, 9.
72. Victoria, *Zen at War*, 183.

Monasteries are not all the same. They have different levels of influence and power. As such, control of the various sects of Buddhism emanates from the higher-grade monasteries in a pyramidal fashion.[73] They also differ in political outlook as well as specializing in something, from trade to sports to centers for learning.[74] They also served in other dual purposes, from being an army headquarters in Thailand to detaining Russian prisoners in Japan.[75] Most monasteries require a minimum number of monks to live there to perform critical ceremonies. In Thailand, the minimum number of monks required is five.[76] Moreover, where Buddhist monks once travelled constantly, never staying too long in one place (as Gautama did), now monks and nuns are encouraged to seek refuge in just one Buddhist monastery. However, if a monk or nun lives in a monastery, they must follow the monastic rules, known as *Vinaya*.

Vinaya

Vinaya is the code of conduct for monks and nuns of *Sanghas*, consisting of two hundred and twenty precepts arranged by categories, that vary among the various Buddhist traditions and schools.[77] These disciplinary rules are oriented for monks and nuns to refrain from worldly affairs, such as foul language, drinking alcohol, sexual activity, to personal affairs, such as bathing only *once every two weeks*.[78] These rules force monks and nuns to live in dependence on the local community. As well, the monastic rules have not been diluted over the centuries by reinterpretation or adaption to changing circumstances.[79]

Transgressions of the *Sangha Vinaya* require punishment of the offending monk or nun, which can include temporary or permanent expulsion from the *Sangha*. According to Lamotte, the discipline which nuns are

---

73. Victoria, *Zen at War*, 4.
74. Jerryson, *Buddhist Fury*, 23.
75. Victoria, *Zen at War*, 63.
76. Jerryson, *Buddhist Fury*, 120.
77. Bechert and Gombrich, eds., *The World of Buddhism*, 56; https://www.wisdom-lib.org/buddhism/book/buddhist-monastic-discipline/d/doc4044.html
78. https://www.wisdomlib.org/buddhism/book/buddhist-monastic-discipline/d/doc4044.html
79. Lehr, *Militant Buddhism*, 57.

subjected to is generally stricter than that of the monks.[80] Finally, regarding suicide, the *Vinaya* condemns it because it is taking a life, which violates the first of the five precepts.[81]

Five Precepts

While the *Vinaya* are the rules monks and nuns live by in a monastery and as members of the *Sangha*, all Buddhists (lay and ordained alike) must also adhere to a personal ethics honor code—known as the five precepts. Unlike *Vinaya*, transgressions of any precept do not necessarily result in any real-world punishment, depending on the severity of the violation. However, monks can expect complete expulsion from the *Sangha* for violating some precepts, such as killing someone, lying, or stealing. Temporary expulsion usually follows for lesser offenses. Sanctions come from the *Sangha* at the assigned monastery. On the other hand, if monks or nuns violate any precepts, it is believed that they can suffer the consequences of negative karma (to be discussed shortly), affecting one's reincarnation.

On the positive side, precepts are meant to develop one's mind and character to make progress towards enlightenment. For lay Buddhists, there are five precepts to follow, while ordained monks and nuns must follow as many as ten precepts—as the minimum standard of Buddhist morality. The first five precepts are:

1. *I will abstain from killing any breathing beings or causing someone else to kill.*

   This precept is based on the Hindu principle of *ahisma* (i.e., non-harming, non-violence). The seriousness of the act of killing which adversely affects reincarnation depends on three factors: 1) size of being killed, 2) being's virtues, and 3) intensity of kill.[82] For monks and nuns, killing a human being is one of four transgressions that are grounds for ex-communication from Buddhism.[83] Under this precept, the Buddha condemned the Hindu practice of animal sacrifice by the Brahmins.

---

80. Bechert and Gombrich, eds., *The World of Buddhism*, 56.
81. Jerryson, *Buddhist Fury*, 19.
82. Lehr, *Militant Buddhism*, 59.
83. Jerryson, *Buddhist Fury*, 18.

Killing for Religion

However, this precept does not apply to kings. One of the most famous kings in Sri Lankan history was Dutugamunu, primarily because he was the first ruler to unify the island in the 2nd century BCE. The *Mahavamsa* chronicle said he placed a Buddhist relic in his spear and went to war along with five hundred monks. After he destroyed the Tamil King Elara and his Hindu kingdom, King Dutugamunu was disconsolate about the significant bloodshed. His Buddhist followers reassured him that the people slain were equivalent to beasts and equaled only one and one-half of a Buddhist. He was told that using violence was acceptable to create peace.[84]

Regarding the military, the Buddha did not allow soldiers to become monks because of this precept.[85] However, the Buddha never attempted to teach *ahisma* to kings as he knew their having a military force was a requirement to rule and maintain the security of society and Buddhism.[86] Finally, the Buddha passionately believed that every action created a reaction (analogous to Newton's third law of motion). So, killing creates a killer; conquering gains an enemy who may conquer you in turn; and he who plunders could be plundered in turn.[87]

2. *I will abstain from taking what is not given.*

According to Peter Harvey, a former professor of Buddhist Studies at the University of Sunderland, this also covers fraud, cheating, forgery, as well as "falsely denying that one is in debt to someone."[88]

3. *I will abstain from sexual misconduct concerning sense-pleasures.*

This generally refers to adultery, as well as rape and incest. It also applies to sex with those who are legally under the protection of a guardian. It can be interpreted in different ways in the varying Buddhist traditions (to be discussed).

4. *I will abstain from false speech.*

---

84. https://www.swarthmore.edu/friends-historical-library/why-religions-facilitate-war-and-how-religions-facilitate-peace
85. Lehr, *Militant Buddhism*, 61–2.
86. Lehr, *Militant Buddhism*, 67.
87. Lehr, *Militant Buddhism*, 66.
88. Harvey, An Introduction to Buddhism, 70.

According to Harvey, this includes "any form of lying, deception or exaggeration...even non-verbal deception by gesture or other indication . . . or misleading statements."[89]

5. *I will abstain from alcoholic drink or drugs.*

According to Harvey, intoxication is perceived as a way to mask the sufferings of life. It is seen as damaging to one's mental clarity, mindfulness, and ability to keep the other four precepts.[90]

There are five more precepts within the *Theravada* tradition that monks and nuns must follow. They include:

1. *I will abstain from sexual activity.*
2. *I will abstain from eating at the wrong time* (afternoon through evening).
3. *I will abstain from jewelry, perfume, and entertainment.*
4. *I will abstain from sleeping on a high bed* (better to sleep on the floor).
5. *I will abstain from accepting money.*[91]

Most Buddhist traditions focus on overcoming human suffering and breaking the cycle of endless death and rebirth. Joys in life are perceived as transient and the world is, in reality, a place of suffering. As such, Buddhism offers everyone salvation from suffering and from the endless cycle of death and rebirth. The foundation of Buddhism begins with the Four Noble Truths.

Four Noble Truths

The Four Noble Truths are (in order): 1) the truth that all life is suffering, 2) the truth that suffering has a cause, 3) the truth that there can be an end to suffering, and 4) the truth that the way to end suffering is to follow the Eightfold Path. Beginning with the First Noble Truth, the ancient Indian word for suffering is *Dukkha* (in Pali, which is an Indo-European language related to Sanskrit) which means "incapable of satisfying."[92] *Dukkha* is the

---

89. Harvey, An Introduction to Buddhism, 72–73.
90. Harvey, An Introduction to Buddhism, 77.
91. https://www.accesstoinsight.org/ptf/dhamma/sila/dasasila.html
92. Lehr, *Militant Buddhism*, 48.

unsatisfactory nature of life, despite any temporary pleasant experiences. Because happiness is temporary as compared to unhappiness, people cannot attain permanent happiness. Suffering ends when craving, desire, and clinging to possessions ceases. Human desire causes suffering, and the Eightfold Path ends all desires (hence, suffering).[93] *Dukkha* is also one of three marks of existence.

The three marks of existence include: 1) *Dukkha*, 2) Impermanence, and 3) Not Soul. *Dukkha* includes the disappointments and dissatisfactions of everyday life. Impermanence is about things in life constantly changing. *Dukkha* and impermanence are ideas also found in other Indian religions, such as Hinduism. Finally, No Soul, also known as *Anatman*, reflects the lack of permanent self or soul, which is not the belief in Christianity or Hinduism. Buddhism is about finding the *Anatman* in oneself. However, Buddhism does believe that a person's quasi-soul or consciousness exists forever.[94]

Regarding the Second Noble Truth, Gautama realized that the causes of suffering are craving, desire, and ignorance. The power of these human shortcomings to cause suffering is the essence of the Second Noble Truth. While these aspects of human shortcomings cause human suffering, the cessation of these causes is the Third Noble Truth. Gautama demonstrated and taught that liberation from attachment to everything would eliminate the possibility of suffering. However, there appears to be a significant disconnect in that monks might "crave" or "desire" to become a Buddha someday and seek merits to achieve this goal – would this not prolong suffering?

The Fourth Noble Truth is the Eightfold Path that leads to *Nirvana*, which is how one is freed from the endless cycle of suffering, dying, and returning to suffer some more. When discussing the Eightfold Path, Gautama put it in the context of taking the *middle way* between the extremes of asceticism and hedonistic pleasures.[95] The Eightfold Path consists of: 1) Right View/Understanding, 2) Right Intention/Thought, 3) Right Speech, 4) Right Action, 5) Right Living, 6) Right Effort, 7) Right Mindfulness, and 8) Right Concentration.[96]

---

93. Bechert and Gombrich, eds., *The World of Buddhism*, 16.

94. De Bary, ed., *Sources of Chinese Tradition Volume 1*, 268; Smith, *The World's Religions*, 115. *Vijnana* (Sanskrit) means a person's consciousness or life force. It is evolving through an infinite continuum.

95. Ford, *Cold War Monks*, 3.

96. Bechert and Gombrich, eds., *The World of Buddhism*, 16.

Buddhist scholars naturally grouped the eight paths under three general headings: Wisdom, Moral Virtues, and Meditation. Wisdom is the main and ultimate aspect of the Eightfold Path.[97] According to the *Dhammapada*, "Happiness is the attainment of wisdom."[98] The two elements that come under the Wisdom heading include Right View/Understanding and Right Intention/Thought. An example of the Right Understanding is one's belief in the Buddhist principles of karma, reincarnation, and the Four Noble Truths. An example of Right Intention would be attaining peaceful renunciation.

The next three elements come under the Moral Virtues heading. It is important to note that sound morality is the basis for liberation from *Samsara* and to achieve *Nirvana* (both to be discussed next).[99] An example of Right Speech is not lying, slandering, or gossiping to or about anyone. An example of Right Action is refraining from killing any living creature, stealing anything, and sexual misconduct, such as adultery.[100] An example of Right Livelihood for monks is living according to the monastic code. Each *Sangha* protects itself by living in the Right Environment, which facilitates the Right Livelihood for monks. Monasteries and their rules exist to help protect the minds of monks and nuns (i.e., Right Thought).[101]

The final three elements come under the Meditation heading. An example of Right Effort is to avoid unwholesome environments that might disrupt quality meditation. An example of Right Mindfulness is not being absent minded and being mindful about the impermanence of the body, emotions, and mind. Finally, an example of Right Concentration is meditating correctly with focus.

The goal of the Eightfold Path is to achieve *Nirvana*.

---

97. Bechert and Gombrich, eds., *The World of Buddhism*, 53.

98. Fronsdal, *The Dhammapada*, 86.

99. https://fpmt.org/mandala/archives/older/mandala-issues-for-1996/september/the-benefits-of-being-monks-and-nuns/

100. Lehr, *Militant Buddhism*, 51.

101. https://fpmt.org/mandala/archives/older/mandala-issues-for-1996/september/the-benefits-of-being-monks-and-nuns/

Nirvana

Nirvana is an ancient Indian word meaning "to release or extinguish."[102] What Buddhists seek to be "released" from is called *Samsara*. *Samsara* refers to the theory of being born into suffering, eventually dying, and then being reborn – a cycle of life, matter, and existence for eternity.[103] It is the foundation of Buddhism, *as it is with all major Indian religions, including Hinduism*. Release from this eternal cycle of suffering is known as *Nirvana*. As such, *Nirvana* is the most important aspect of Buddhism, and *any* Buddhist may achieve *Nirvana*.

So, how does one achieve *Nirvana*? To begin, what binds one to the endless cycle of rebirth is desire, which rests upon a false perception of one's condition in life.[104] To eliminate desire and attain *Nirvana*, one must purify the mind, restrain and refrain from any appetites, and be generous and kind.[105] The state of *Nirvana*, as described in Buddhist texts, is one of complete liberation, enlightenment, happiness, freedom, and permanence. *Nirvana* is the ending of desire, hence, the end of suffering.[106] When Buddhists attain *Nirvana*, a corpse is all that remains upon death, and they can do no more for humanity.[107] In *Nirvana*, there is no consciousness to be reborn.[108]

However, there are major logjams that prevent most Buddhists from achieving *Nirvana*, such as politics and social works.[109] Peter Lehr, a research fellow at the University of St Andrews, cited a metaphor from an abbot from Mandalay, Myanmar, that a Buddhist's efforts to reach *Nirvana* are like being a log in a river. If it encounters little to no obstacles, it will eventually reach the ocean (i.e., *Nirvana*). However, politics is an obstacle in the river that can cause the log to become waterlogged and eventually to sink. Instead of reaching the ocean, the log ends up on the bottom (in hell).[110]

102. Fronsdal, *The Dhammapada*, xxii.
103. Bechert and Gombrich, eds., *The World of Buddhism*, 48.
104. Bechert and Gombrich, eds., *The World of Buddhism*, 9.
105. Bechert and Gombrich, eds., *The World of Buddhism*, 9, 49.
106. Bechert and Gombrich, eds., *The World of Buddhism*, 51; Jerryson, *Buddhist Fury*, 19.
107. Bechert and Gombrich, eds., *The World of Buddhism*, 41, 44.
108. De Bary, *Sources of Chinese Tradition Volume 1*, 268.
109. Lehr, *Militant Buddhism*, 256.
110. Lehr, *Militant Buddhism*, 108.

The main problem regarding *Nirvana* is *Samsara*. Most Asian Buddhist laypeople do *not* want to be "extinguished" forever. In fact, they generally like the idea of coming back in a better position in life. It appeals to the competitive nature of people more than the belief that everyone is suffering and will always be suffering. While such suffering may have been more common in Gautama's era (around the middle of the 6th century BCE), that is generally not the case thousands of years later. According to World Bank data, in 1990, almost two billion people lived in *extreme poverty* (hence, likely to be suffering). Of the two billion people, around one and a half billion of them lived in South and East Asia (where Buddhism is prevalent). By 2015 (*just 25 years later*), most people living in extreme poverty lived only in sub-Saharan Africa and no longer in Asia.[111] According to Kevin Trainor, a professor specializing in South Asian Buddhist traditions at the University of Vermont, most Asian Buddhist followers sought better rebirth through merit and belief in *Dharma*. They were not interested in achieving *Nirvana* and freedom from *Samsara*.[112] The people Gautama was reaching out to were suffering from lust and cravings; experiencing misery and pain; were arrogant, deceitful, and insincere; maintained dull faculties and little wisdom, and were arrogant and obsessed with appearances.[113] Today, these characteristics apply to only a small minority of people in Asian society.

Merit

As previously discussed, *Samsara* is the endless cycle of birth, life, death, and rebirth. (Note that what is actually going through these endless life cycles is a person's *vijnana* –consciousness or life force.) Merit is a critical aspect of rebirth. Rebirth depends on merits or demerits gained by one's own karma (to be discussed next) or accrued from family member donations (known as "merit transfers"). In fact, merit can even be transferred to the dead – called "ancestor veneration." This means a dead person can achieve Buddhahood! As well, a dead ancestor's plight can adversely affect the living, so ancestor veneration is very important.[114]

---

111. https://ourworldindata.org/extreme-poverty

112. Keown, *Buddhism*, 60–63, 74–85, 185–187.

113. Shinozaki, Ziporyn, and Earhart, Translators, *The Threefold Lotus Sutra*, 72, 79, 81.

114. Shinozaki, Ziporyn, and Earhart, Translators, *The Threefold Lotus Sutra*, xvii.

The primary purpose for ancestor veneration is to do one's filial duty, to show devotion and respect, and to look after ancestors in their afterlives by providing offerings of food and other provisions. Some family members may visit the graves of their parents or other ancestors, leave flowers and pray to them in order to honor and remember them, while also asking their deceased ancestors to continue to look after them. This act of ancestor worship does not confer any belief that the departed ancestors have become any kind of deity. This social phenomenon appears in some form in all human cultures and most religions.

The way to gain merit for lay Buddhists is to have good intentions during life; live ethically; donate food, funds, or gifts to monks, nuns, or monasteries; build temples; support the local *Sangha*; and the like.[115] A new temple is thought to win more merit for the builder than the maintenance of an old temple. (Hence, the proliferation of temples in Buddhist countries.)[116] Because society was agrarian, *Sanghas* often received land for merit. As a result, they often owned the land that other people worked on. As such, *Sanghas* became major feudal landlords in the 9-12th centuries![117]

Generosity, as demonstrated by such gifts, is considered the basis of morality. The more generous one is in spirit, the purer one's mind becomes.[118] The way to gain merit for monks is to preserve and spread the *dharma* everywhere for the good of the world. The *bodhisattva* ("Buddha-to-be" in the *Mahayana* tradition) accumulates merits by practicing six perfections: 1) generosity, 2) morality, 3) patience, 4) vigor, 5) meditation, and 6) wisdom.[119] The more merit accumulated during one's lifetime influences how well one is reborn. Merit can secure a place in heaven or a more prosperous reincarnation.[120] Each rebirth takes place within one of (at most) six realms depending on how much merit one has acquired: heaven, demi-gods, humans, animals, ghosts, or hell.[121] The various traditions and schools within Buddhism have not agreed on what exactly is reborn (likely

---

115. Bechert and Gombrich, eds., *The World of Buddhism*, 14; Lehr, *Militant Buddhism*, 91.
116. Bechert and Gombrich, eds., *The World of Buddhism*, 124.
117. Bechert and Gombrich., eds., *The World of Buddhism*, 136.
118. Smith, *The World's Religions*, 14.
119. Bechert and Gombrich, eds., *The World of Buddhism*, 91.
120. Smith, *The World's Religions*, 14.
121. Bechert and Gopmbrich, eds., *The World of Buddhism*, 134.

consciousness), how many realms of rebirth there are (five or six); or how quickly rebirth occurs after death.[122]

The following quotes regarding merit are taken from an English translation of the *Dhammapada*:

"One who makes merit rejoices in this life; Rejoices in the next."[123]

"When one is slow to make merit, One's mind delights in evil. Merit piled up brings happiness."[124]

"Evildoers are reborn in hell, People of good conduct go to heaven."[125]

"Those who take up wrong views, Go to a bad rebirth."[126]

"Happiness is merit at the end of one's life."[127]

Karma

Karma (a Sanskrit word) is a core belief in Buddhism, though it originated from the Vedic religion, the foundation of Hinduism. Essentially, if one does good things, then good things will happen to that person – and vice versa. If one does bad things, then bad things will happen to that person. However, karma is more than doing various deeds. It is one's intent when doing them that is critical. The intent is essential to bring about a karmic consequence. In fact, one can accumulate karma without any physical actions. Just having good or bad thoughts creates karmic seeds. Karma is where the intent of actions taken by an individual can influence that person's future *and future rebirth*. So, good deeds done with good intent result in good karma and better rebirth, while bad deeds done with bad intent result in bad karma and poorer rebirth.[128] According to Lamotte, Buddha defined karma as *intention*; whether the intention manifested itself in physical, vocal, or mental form, it was the intention alone that had a

---

122. Bechert and Gopmbrich, eds., *The World of Buddhism*, 48.
123. Fronsdal, *The Dhammapada*, 4.
124. Fronsdal, *The Dhammapada*, 31.
125. Fronsdal, *The Dhammapada*, 33.
126. Fronsdal, *The Dhammapada*, 81.
127. Fronsdal, *The Dhammapada*, 86.
128. Olivelle, *Upanishads*, xlvii, 202.

moral character: good, bad, or neutral.[129] Karma is directly related to merit; hence, it affects one's existence in *samsara*. Regarding religion and conflict, Buddhists believe that violence leads to negative karmic consequences such that slain warriors on the battlefield are reincarnated as animals or even in hell.[130] In Hinduism, karma is perceived to be a force of justice that compels believers to behave according to *dharma*.[131] Because of karma, *everyone gets what they deserve*.[132]

Buddhist Traditions

The twelve Hebrew tribes split into Israel and Judah; Christendom split into the Eastern and Western churches; the Western church split into Catholicism and Protestantism; and Protestantism split into numerous more sects. As such, it is not unusual to have Buddhism split into different schools and traditions.[133] As Buddhism evolved, different variations of it evolved that are referred to as "traditions." Just as Hinduism evolved into many doctrinal schools, Buddhism did something similar. During the last centuries of the 1st millennium BCE, various Buddhist schools of thought were recognized, each with its own set of sacred texts. The doctrinal schools coalesced into two primary traditions – *Theravada* and *Mahayana* Buddhism, and into a subset of the *Mahayana* tradition known as *Vajrayana* Buddhism.

Today, most Buddhists generally classify themselves as either *Theravada* or *Mahayana*. *Theravada* translates to "School of Elders," while *Mahayana* translates to "The Great Vehicle" ("yana" means vehicle towards enlightenment). In these two Buddhist tradition conceptions, one crosses a river in a vehicle to reach *Nirvana*, and then abandons the vehicle once arrived. In *Theravada*, very few people can be carried across, while in *Mahayana*, far more people can use the vehicle and be carried by it. Both these Buddhist traditions hold the Four Noble Truths as their core principle, though beyond that they have unique doctrines and practices.[134] Xue Yu, a

129. Bechert and Gombrich, eds., *The World of Buddhism*, 51.
130. Tikhonov and Brekke, eds., *Buddhism and Violence*, 7.
131. https://berkleycenter.georgetown.edu/essays/karma-hinduism
132. Smith, *The World's Religions*, 64.
133. Smith, *The World's Religions*, 120. It is interesting to note that there are more schools, traditions, sects, and denominations within Buddhism than there are within Christianity.
134. Jerryson, *Buddhist Fury*, 5.

professor at Chinese University in Hong Kong, determined that, in the end, it was left for Buddhists to decide which tradition to follow – *Theravada* or *Mahayana*.[135]

Each tradition is practiced in separate areas of the world. *Theravada* Buddhism has spread into the rural areas of mainland Southeast Asia (displacing *Mahayana* Buddhism and Hinduism), including Sri Lanka, Burma, Laos, Thailand, Cambodia, Vietnam, Malaysia, and Bangladesh. The *Mahayana* Buddhist tradition is mainly followed in Northeast and Central Asia, including China, Vietnam, Korea, and Japan. Finally, *Vajrayana* is found in Japan, Tibet, Mongolia, and the USA.[136] Finally, *Theravada* Buddhism remained a relatively unified tradition in contrast to *Mahayana* Buddhism, which divided again into a number of denominations or schools.[137]

Theravada Buddhism

Theravada Buddhism is the oldest Buddhist tradition going back at least 2,250 years (*Mahayana* Buddhism dates back only to the 1st century BCE).[138] It stresses withdrawing from the world, including politics.[139] It traces back to the Third Buddhist Council convened around 250 BCE under the patronage of Emperor Ashoka.[140] It began in southern India and eventually spread to Sri Lanka sometime in the 3rd century BCE by Ashoka's son, Mahendra.[141] By the 11th century, it had spread from Sri Lanka to the entire Southeast Asian mainland. The *Theravada* tradition considers itself the more orthodox form of Buddhism, with a more conservative and monastic discipline than the *Mahayana* tradition. The *Theravada* tradition adopted the *Tripitaka*, known as the Pali Canon of the *Theravada* School.[142] The *Tripitaka* was transmitted to Sri Lanka and eventually written down in

---

135. Tikhonov and Brekke, eds., *Buddhism and Violence*, 204.
136. https://hwpi.harvard.edu/files/pluralism/files/vajrayana-the_diamond_vehicle_1.pdf
137. Smith, *The World's Religions*, 128.
138. Lehr, *Militant Buddhism*, 33.
139. Almond, Appleby, and Sivan, *Strong Religion*, 165.
140. Lehr, *Militant Buddhism*, 33.
141. Bechert and Gombrich, eds., *The World of Buddhism*, 60.
142. Note that the Pali Canon is the only complete Buddhist canon surviving in the Pali language.

29 BCE – *454 years after Gautama died*! The *Theravada* tradition follows the teachings of the Buddha in the framework of the Four Noble Truths.

In *Theravada* Buddhism, a Buddha is someone who can be enlightened by their own efforts and insights, much like Gautama in the 6th century BCE. However, in the *Theravada* tradition, the goal of the eightfold path is the perfect person, but not necessarily Buddhahood.[143]

An *arhat* in Theravada Buddhism is someone who has achieved near-perfection and is only waiting to die to then pass into *Nirvana*. This is not the same as Buddhahood, but it is as close as most humans can get. Gautama showed everyone how to achieve *Nirvana*. However, *Theravada* sees Gautama as the only Buddha in the current era. (In this tradition, a new Buddha appears every five thousand years.[144]) As well, *Theravada* Buddhists view Gautama the Buddha as a teacher and not a deity.[145]

Theravada Buddhism is a unified system of beliefs and practices to include animistic forms of worship.[146] There are three monastic rules of *Theravada* Buddhism, which are: 1) simplicity, 2) no killing, and 3) celibacy. As well, there are three principles: 1) refrain from doing evil, 2) do good, and 3) benefit humanity.[147] However, *Theravada* Buddhism has transformed into a militant, ultra-nationalist tradition that is on the rise in Southeast Asia. This latest interpretation Buddhism allows violent actions in defense of the religion.[148]

Mahayana Buddhism

Mahayana ("Greater Vehicle") refers to all forms of Buddhism, which consider the *Mahayana Sutras* as the authoritative scriptures and accurate rendering of Buddha's words. The *Mahayana* tradition has been a more liberal form of Buddhism, allowing different and new interpretations over time. The *Sutras* are believed to contain the original teachings of the Buddha and are based on the Sanskrit canon written between the 1st century BCE and the 1st century CE. Because *Theravada* Buddhism is based on the Pali

---

143. Lehr, *Militant Buddhism*, 49.
144. Parrinder, *World Religions*, 262.
145. Lehr, *Militant Buddhism*, 16.
146. Lehr, *Militant Buddhism*, 16.
147. Tikhonov and Brekke, eds., *Buddhism and Violence*, 197.
148. Gunasingham, "Buddhist Extremism in Sri Lanka and Myanmar," 1; Lehr, *Militant Buddhism*, 2.

canon (which is considered more pure and true to Buddhism), *Mahayana* Buddhism (based on Sanskrit canon) is perceived as corrupted.[149] Besides recording Buddha's insights, the *Mahayana Sutras* also included expanded cosmologies and mythologies as well as new spiritual practices and ideas.

Initially, the *Mahayana* tradition was just a small movement struggling to expand. During the 5th and 6th centuries CE, the *Mahayana* following increased significantly, though still a minority compared to other Buddhist schools. Perhaps one reason for this is that the *Mahayana* tradition did not form a separate school or sect of Buddhism or even establish a separate monastic code (i.e., *Vinaya*). Records indicate that both *Mahayana* and non-*Mahayana* monks lived together in the same monasteries. The key difference was that *Mahayana* monks worshipped and strived to become *bodhisattvas* while the other monks did not. Today, *Mahayana* Buddhists represent approximately two-thirds of the total Buddhist population worldwide, most living in East Asia.

Followers of the *Mahayana* tradition claim they follow Buddha's more profound, more advanced doctrines, reserved for those who follow the *bodhisattva* path. *Bodhisattva* means "Being of Wisdom" or "Being Bound for Awakening" and refers to one who is on the path to Buddhahood.[150] As such, a *bodhisattva* is one who will eventually become a Buddha. (The female version is referred to as *mahasattva*.) The term *Mahayana* was originally a synonym for "*Bodhisattva* Vehicle." So, *Mahayana* Buddhism is based upon the path to becoming a *bodhisattva*, which is promoted as the highest and most worthwhile endeavor.[151]

According to all Buddhist traditions (to include *Theravada*), to be considered a *bodhisattva*, one has to make a vow and receive confirmation on one's future Buddhahood. So, *bodhisattvas* are Buddhas-to-be who have chosen to delay entry into *Nirvana* to remain on earth to help humanity.[152] Interestingly, a critical duty of any *bodhisattva* is to commit the sin of killing to prevent others from having to do so. The thinking is that *bodhisattvas* are already promised *Nirvana* where everyone else is not – and, therefore if others kill, they will suffer in rebirth (see *Samsara*).[153] As such, *bodhisat-*

---

149. Victoria, *Zen at War*, 14.
150. The Dalai Lama is a real-world and well-known example of a bodhisattva. (Smith, *The World's Religions*, 143)
151. Bechert and Gombrich, eds., *The World of Buddhism*, 41, 43.
152. Smith, *The World's Religions*, 91.
153. Jerryson, *Buddhist Fury*, 43–4.

tvas have a spiritual *license to kill*. Unlike *Theravada* Buddhism, the result of the eightfold path in *Mahayana* Buddhism is full Buddhahood.[154] *Mahayana* Buddhism is practiced today in China, Japan, Korea, and Vietnam. It includes the Pure Land, Zen, Nichiren, Shingon, and Tendai Buddhism schools found throughout East Asia.

Vajrayana Buddhism

Vajrayana Buddhism ("Diamond Vehicle") is a subset of *Mahayana* Buddhism. It was begun by Guru Padmasambhava in Tibet around 767 CE. *Vajrayana* spread to East Asia, Mongolia, and later to Russia, Europe, and America. It began during the Gupta Empire in India with the development of a new class of Buddhist literature called the *Tantras*. By the 8th century, the *Tantric* tradition was very influential in India. The *Tantras* focused on mantras, meditation, body positions, drinking alcohol, and performing sexual rituals. In fact, *Tantra* and sex are pretty much synonymous. Sexual energy is understood to permeate the cosmos; thus, tapping into it is tapping into the most basic forces of cosmic essence and creativity. Finally, sexual practice must be done under the supervision of a guru.[155]

The *Tantra* system is thought to be the quickest way to *Nirvana*, the most rapid means to salvation. Under the Guptas, *Tantric* Buddhism became integrated into the *Vajrayana* tradition. As it stands today, the *Mahayana* tradition has 360 million followers, *Theravada* has less than half of that at 150 million adherents. *Vajrayana* only has around 18 million followers.[156]

---

154. Lehr, *Militant Buddhism*, 49.
155. Smith, *The World's Religions*, 141.
156. Harvey, An Introduction to Buddhism, 3.

BUDDHISM

Map of China[157]

Pure Land Buddhism

Instead of various "traditions" of Buddhism found in India, various "sects" formed in Japan (over the 1,500 years that Buddhism has existed there[158]), the most common being Pure Land, Zen, and Nichiren.[159] Pure Land Buddhism (also known as *Shingon* and *Amidism*) is a broad branch of *Mahayana* Buddhism and one of the most widely practiced sects of Buddhism in East Asia. It was introduced into Japan during the Heian Period (794-1185 CE) by *Bodhisattva* Kukai (of the Mount Koya monastery) after studying Buddhism in Xian, China, beginning in 804 CE (see map of China). Pure Land Buddhists believed that all the faithful *Shingonists* who died would go to the "pure land" (also known as the *Western Paradise*).[160] *All believers would receive salvation and go to heaven.*[161] Pure Land Buddhism was first developed in India around the 2nd century BCE and spread to China by the

---

157. CIA World Factbook, https://www.riddle.ru/mirrors/factbook2001/geos/ch.html

158. Victoria, *Zen at War*, 3.

159. https://www.buddha101.com/h_japan.htm

160. Barton, "Buddhism and Shinto: The Two Pillars of Japanese Culture," https://japanology.org/2016/06/buddhism-and-shinto-the-two-pillars-of-japanese-culture/

161. Parrinder, *World Religions,* 366; Langley, *World Religions,* 46.

2nd century CE. It spread to Japan by the 6th century CE, and it is now the most widely practiced form of Buddhism in Japan.[162]

Zen Buddhism

Zen means *meditation*—an essential feature of Buddhism from ancient India.[163] Zen emphasizes that all human beings possess the Buddha-nature within themselves and need only the actual experience of it to achieve enlightenment. Enlightenment is seen as a liberation from one's intellectual nature, from the burden of fixed ideas and feelings about reality.[164] Training and practice to achieve this enlightenment come from the practical instruction of a Zen Master.[165] It is believed that this instruction can awaken the Buddha-nature that everyone possesses within themselves. Training is conducted in a large meditation hall where the lotus posture (adopted from India) is practiced.[166] Zen also teaches self-understanding and self-reliance.[167]

Zen Buddhism is a form of Chinese *Mahayana* Buddhism influenced heavily by concepts from Daoism, that was introduced to Japan by Priest Eisai of China at the beginning of the Kamakura period (1135-1333 CE).[168] As the meditation school of Buddhism, it became the most influential stream of Buddhism throughout Asia.[169] Zen became widely popular in Japan, with Zen temples built throughout the country.[170] Eisai believed that Zen Buddhism would be able to help protect Japan. Zen influenced both the martial arts and the military class in Japan.[171]

To most people, Zen Buddhism is about discovering one's inner serenity and social peace. However, Zen advocates taking a sword to demons as it is perceived as good to kill evil and preserve the true *dharma*.[172] In other words, it believes in the humane killing of one person so that many may

---

162. Skilton, *A Concise History of Buddhism*, 104.
163. De Bary, ed., *Sources of Japanese Tradition Volume I*, 226.
164. Smith, *The World's Religions*, 132.
165. Smith, *The World's Religions*, 132.
166. Smith, *The World's Religions*, 133.
167. De Bary, *Sources of Japanese Tradition*, 226.
168. Davies, *Japanese Culture*, 90, 98; Victoria, *Zen at War*, 99.
169. Davies, *Japanese Culture*, 90.
170. Davies, *Japanese Culture*, 91.
171. Davies, *Japanese Culture*, 92.
172. Ford, *Cold War Monks*, 16, 17; Victoria, *Zen at War*, 92.

live.[173] Regarding war, Zen Buddhism did not see it as either inherently good or bad.[174]

The Samurai followed *Bushido*, an honor code that guided their lives. *Bushido* is thought to be a combination of Zen Buddhism and Confucianism.[175] *Bushido* had eight major characteristics to include: 1) fervent loyalty, 2) esteem for military prowess, 3) spirit of self-sacrifice, 4) realism, 5) self-reliance, 6) esteem for order, 7) respect for truthfulness and ambition, and 8) simplicity in life.[176] According to Victoria, the reason *Bushido* developed so extensively in Japan was due to Zen. It was thought that the power from Zen training could be converted into *Bushido*, hence, into military power.[177] In the 1930s and 1940s, Zen was hijacked by the Meiji regime and modified to support the war effort. All Japanese men were expected to uphold the *Bushido* code and self-sacrifice themselves in war on behalf of the emperor and the country.[178] This *New Buddhism* was founded on a militarized Zen that required absolute loyalty to the emperor.[179] It was believed that the Bushido spirit was critical to overcoming a better-equipped and numerically-superior enemy.[180]

Sacred Texts

Unlike Hinduism, Buddhism does not have a holy book or sacred text that the various Buddhist traditions all agree on.[181] Gautama wrote nothing during his lifetime.[182] Like all Indian religions, Buddhism began as an oral tradition in ancient times, usually in an Indo-Aryan language such as Pali. Buddhist literature (like the *Qur'an*) is very repetitive, which facilitates

---

173. Victoria, *Zen at War*, 87.
174. Victoria, *Zen at War*, 88.
175. Davies, *Japanese Culture*, 92. Confucianism is analogous to Hinduism in India. It originated in ancient China as a philosophy, religion, way of governing, and way of life.
176. Victoria, *Zen at War*, 103.
177. Victoria, *Zen at War*, 98, 99.
178. Victoria, *Zen at War*, 104, 105.
179. Victoria, *Zen at War*, 114.
180. Victoria, *Zen at War*, 114.
181. Jerryson, *Buddhist Fury*, 5.
182. Smith, *The World's Religions*, 112.

recitation and memorization.[183] Gombrich observed that "The importance of communal recitation in Buddhist history cannot be overstated."[184] Historically, Buddhism has evolved during the Iron Age in northern India (between 1300 – 300 BCE). It was also during this time that the sacred Hindu texts, the *Upanishads*, were being disseminated. Gautama was likely taught about the *Upanishads*, which undoubtedly affected his beliefs.

The earliest sacred scriptures were resident in the Buddhist schools in Southeast Asia. The first Buddhist sacred texts were recorded in Sri Lanka about 150 years after Gautama died.[185] The first printing of the whole Buddhist Canon was done in 972 CE.[186] Theravadan monks were responsible for writing and preserving the scriptures (in Sanskrit) using three categories: 1) canonical, 2) commentarial, and 3) pseudo-canonical. The eldest Buddhist monks were responsible for the canonical writings.[187] Buddhist literature, like many of the oral traditions, is very repetitive, which helps in memorization.[188] As with the Bible, there were many edits, redactions, and outright changes to these holy scriptures.[189] According to Michio Shinozaki, president of the Rissho Kosei-kai Gakurin Seminary in Tokyo, "Every classic [like the *Lotus Sutra*] has to be reborn according to the demands of the times."[190] This writing of Buddhist literature led to the implementation of writing in many Asian cultures, from Tibet to Japan.[191]

Tripitaka

Each of the multiple schools of Buddhism maintained its preferred sacred texts. For the *Theravada* school, various texts written in Pali were combined and referred to as the *Tripitaka* – meaning the triple baskets of Discipline,

---

183. Smith, *The World's Religions*, 80.
184. Bechert and Gombrich, eds., *The World of Buddhism*, 81.
185. Smith, *The World's Religions*, 112.
186. Bechert and Gombrich, eds., *The World of Buddhism*, 204.
187. Bechert and Gombrich, eds., *The World of Buddhism*, 77, 79.
188. Bechert and Gombrich, eds., *The World of Buddhism*, 80.
189. See the seven ecumenical councils recognized by both the Eastern Orthodox and Roman Catholic Churches.
190. Shinozaki, Ziporyn, and Earhart, translators, *The Threefold Lotus Sutra*, xxiii.
191. Bechert and Gombrich, eds., *The World of Buddhism*, 258.

Sayings, and Philosophy. The general tenets of *Theravada* Buddhism are found in the *Tripitaka*.[192]

Dhammapada

Another famous and perhaps the most beloved sacred text in Buddhism is the *Dhammapada*, a collection of poetic verses encompassing the core teachings of the Buddha from the earliest period in India.[193] For thousands of years, Buddhists memorized and chanted the *Dhammapada*.[194] (It was first introduced to the modern world during the second half of the 19th century.[195]) The verses were written in Pali and adapted from poetry, songs, and teachings already current in ancient India *before* Buddhism.[196] The *Dhammapada* is embedded in the second basket (i.e., Sayings) of the *Tripitaka*.[197] It was crafted to be a dichotomy between good and evil.[198] It claimed that if one leads an evil violent life, then in hell is where one's rebirth would be.[199] Its main message is not to attach oneself to anything in one's world.

As noted previously, there have been many changes to the *Dhammapada* for various reasons, from translations to editing.[200] For example, in various versions of the sacred text, chapters and verses appear in a different order.[201] According to Gil Fronsdal, a Zen priest and teacher at the Insight Meditation Center (IMC) of Redwood City, California, "The surviving records do not reveal when any of the existing Dhammapada texts . . . attained their present form."[202]

---

192. Fronsdal, *The Dhammapada*, 109.
193. Fronsdal, *The Dhammapada*, ix.
194. Fronsdal, *The Dhammapada*, ix.
195. Fronsdal, *The Dhammapada*, xi.
196. Fronsdal, *The Dhammapada*, xix.
197. Fronsdal, *The Dhammapada*, xix–xxix, 109.
198. Fronsdal, *The Dhammapada*, xxiv.
199. Fronsdal, *The Dhammapada*, xxi, 33.
200. Fronsdal, *The Dhammapada*, xii.
201. Fronsdal, *The Dhammapada*, 113.
202. Fronsdal, *The Dhammapada*, 111.

Lotus Sutra

The *Lotus Sūtra* (*sutra* meaning "scripture") is one of the most popular and the holiest text in the *Mahayana* tradition.[203] "Lotus Sutra" means "One Buddha Vehicle." The *Lotus Sutra* contains the *final* teachings of Gautama. This *Sutra* is meant to be recited to deepen faith, to gain merit, and to meditate.[204] It is a revolutionary reversal of many of the fundamental doctrines in the *Mahayana* tradition, such as the purpose of life being to reach *Nirvana*. It teaches that all students of Buddha are *bodhisattvas* ("enlightened beings"), whereas in the *Theravada* tradition, there is only one *bodhisattva* alive at any one time. The *Sutra* benefits all living beings and comes from the dwelling place of all buddhas.[205] The critical aspects of the *Lotus Sutra* are *One Dharma* – having no attributes; and the *Great Vehicle Sutra of Innumerable Meanings* – all things are inherently tranquil and empty.[206]

Proselytizing Buddhism

For the last forty-five years of his life, Gautama proselytized his enlightened beliefs. He encouraged his followers to do the same – spread the Buddhist *dharma*.[207] Gautama sent the first sixty monks out to give the gift of the *dharma* to others.[208] However, for three centuries, Buddhism did not spread very far in India. The various languages throughout India and Asia presented the greatest obstacle to propagating the Buddhist faith by missionaries and traders.[209] Then, the Mauryan Empire's third Emperor, Ashoka the Great (304-232 BCE), adopted the religion for himself and his empire in eastern India. The Mauryans ruled over the largest empire in India for over one hundred years.[210] One of the major military efforts by Ashoka was the Kalinga War fought around 261 BCE against the state of

---

203. Bechert and Gombrich, eds., *The World of Buddhism*, 215.
204. Shinozaki, Ziporyn, and Earhart, translators, *The Threefold Lotus Sutra*, xv.
205. Shinozaki, Ziporyn, and Earhart, translators, *The Threefold Lotus Sutra*, xxvii, xxviii, 22.
206. Shinozaki, Ziporyn, and Earhart, translators, *The Threefold Lotus Sutra*, 14, 17, 19.
207. Lehr, *Militant Buddhism*, 36.
208. Smith, *The World's Religions*, 77.
209. Bechert and Gombrich, eds., *The World of Buddhism*, 101.
210. Bechert and Gombrich, eds., *The World of Buddhism*, 82.

Kalinga, an independent feudal kingdom located on the east coast of India (see book cover for an artistic interpretation of one of the battles). It was a very bloody war with nearly 200,000 Indians killed.[211]

Ashoka built numerous temples, monasteries, and stone edifices throughout India and then sent numerous Buddhist emissaries to various countries throughout Central and West Asia and even to ancient Athens in Greece and Alexandria in Egypt. Even after converting to Buddhism, Ashoka maintained an army as well as a death penalty for criminals – which included killing his own wife.[212] Not surprisingly, Ashoka called himself the *Dharma King* while maintaining a great deal of power over the *Sangha*—as demonstrated by his defrocking of around sixty thousand *Sangha* members.[213]

Buddhism was often spread by missionaries and by traders. During Emperor Ashoka's rule, *Theravada* Buddhism spread into Southeast Asia, including Sri Lanka, Burma, Thailand, and Cambodia. Gombrich noted that it was Sri Lanka and not India that became the first Buddhist state, and it has remained so through today.[214] In the end, Ashoka did more than anyone else to spread Buddhism, much like the Apostle Paul did with Christianity.[215]

A couple of centuries later, Kanishka the Great (127-150 CE), an emperor of the Kushan Dynasty in India, also adopted Buddhism for himself and his empire. The Kushan Empire (30-375 CE) controlled the Silk Road trade route. The Kushans proselytized Buddhism throughout their lands and along the Silk Road to Central and South Asia and into China by the 1st or 2nd century CE. As such, the Kushans are most responsible for expanding Buddhism into a global religion (at that time). Of note, according to Geoffrey Parrinder, a Methodist minister and professor at King's College in London, Buddhism was not spread by armed force as the other global religions were.[216]

Buddhism was at its apex in India from 210 BCE to 500 CE.[217] However, as Islam flourished as a new global religion, it displaced Buddhism

---

211. http://indiansaga.com/history/magadha_kalinga.html
212. Victoria, *Zen at War*, 197, 198.
213. Victoria, *Zen at War*, 198, 199.
214. Bechert and Gombrich, eds., *The World of Buddhism*, 83.
215. Bechert and Gombrich, eds., *The World of Buddhism*, 83.
216. Parrinder, *World Religions*, 303.
217. Bechert and Gombrich, eds., *The World of Buddhism*, 60.

in Central Asia beginning in the 10th century CE with the establishment of the Ghaznavid Kingdom. Islamic invasions of India during the 10th to 12th centuries damaged and destroyed many Buddhist institutions.[218] Islam replaced Buddhism in India by the 13th century CE. Muslim armies also conquered Persia, Afghanistan, and most of Central Asia, spreading Islam even further.[219]

As China had other more established religions by the 1st century CE, it took a while for Buddhism to become rooted there. It eventually achieved virtually equal status with Confucianism and Daoism by the 3rd century CE. Various traditions of Buddhism flourished in China, including Pure Land and Zen Buddhism. Emperor Wen of Sui, the Universal Monarch, unified China using Buddhism in 589 CE.[220] Buddhism peaked in China at the end of the Tang Dynasty (960-1279 CE). Han Yu, a government official of the Tang Dynasty, rejected Daoism and Buddhism in 824 CE because they were not Chinese in origin.[221] Emperor Wu-tsung had over forty-four thousand and six hundred monasteries demolished, temple land confiscated, metal Buddha statues melted down, and almost two hundred and sixty thousand monks and nuns forced back into secular life. These moves served as the initial poison leading to the eventual decline of Buddhism in China.[222]

During the 4th century CE, Buddhism spread to Korea (i.e., King Seong of the Baekje Kingdom) and then into Japan during the 6th century CE. King Seong sent a mission to visit the Japanese Emperor Kinmei in 552 CE that included Buddhist monks and texts. From the 8th century onward, Buddhism spread to Tibet and Mongolia.[223] Buddhism was primarily disseminated through traders and monks, though in some cases, it was the result of war. After Japan annexed Korea in 1910, significant efforts were made to replace Korean culture with Japanese culture, including Buddhism.

---

218. Bechert and Gombrich, eds., *The World of Buddhism*, 10; Smith, *The World's Religions*, 78.

219. Bechert and Gombrich, eds., *The World of Buddhism*, 60.

220. Victoria, *Zen at War*, 201.

221. Roy, *Hinduism and the Ethics of Warfare in South Asia*, 371.

222. Victoria, *Zen at War*, 202.

223. Bechert and Gombrich, eds., *The World of Buddhism*, 10; Smith, *The World's Religions*, 78.

Japanese Buddhist priests were conscripted into the military to help evangelize Buddhism and assist in pacification efforts throughout Korea.[224]

A number of events and social factors led to the demise of Buddhism across Asia. It seemed to fade as feudalism, with its kings and kingdoms, was replaced by states.[225] As well, the local *Sanghas* had become corrupt, degenerate, and socially degraded.[226] According to Erik Zurcher, a professor of the history of East Asia at the Leiden University, official proclamations referred to "Buddhism as to something close to 'opium for the people.' In popular literature monks and nuns are usually described as greedy and ignorant, and monasteries as places of corruption."[227]

In India, as *Mahayana* Buddhism became more and more indistinguishable from Hinduism, its usefulness waned, and it began disappearing from India.[228] Then, there were the numerous Muslim invasions into India beginning in 1000 CE.[229] Lamotte wrote that "The Muslim invasions into India, sacking the monasteries, substantially destroyed Buddhist culture by the 13th century, though vestiges remained in India till nearly 1500 CE."[230] By the 17th century, Muslim forces had replaced Buddhism in Turkestan, Malaysia, Indonesia, and Java as well.[231] By the 19th century, Buddhism in China was in a state of malaise, aggravated by corruption and internal rebellions. Its decline was also due to the resurgence of Confucianism, a native philosophical religion.[232] In summary, Victoria observed that,

> Buddhism in India collapsed due to the nature of Indian culture. It collapsed in China because it was contrary to its history and nature of the state. The reason it was able to develop in Japan was completely due to the imperial household. Since the emperor was the state, and Buddhism and the state were one, the emperor and Buddhism were also one.[233]

---

224. Victoria, *Zen at War*, 64, 65.
225. Jerryson and Juergensmeyer, eds., *Buddhist Warfare*, 36.
226. Jerryson and Juergensmeyer, eds., *Buddhist Warfare*, 128.
227. Bechert and Gombrich, eds., *The World of Buddhism*, 208.
228. Parrinder, *World Religions*, 287.
229. Bechert and Gombrich, eds., *The World of Buddhism*, 107, 78.
230. Bechert and Gombrich, eds., *The World of Buddhism*, 60.
231. Bechert and Gombrich, eds., *The World of Buddhism*, 273.
232. Bechert and Gombrich, eds., *The World of Buddhism*, 206.
233. Victoria, *Zen at War*, 82.

Today, China still has the largest number of Buddhist followers, at around 246 million people (18 percent of its population), while Japan has the third largest number (after Thailand) with 84 million Buddhists. Most of these Buddhists follow the *Mahayana* tradition. *Theravada* Buddhism is the dominant religion in Myanmar (i.e., Burma), Cambodia, Tibet, Laos, Mongolia, Thailand, and Sri Lanka. (The latter two countries maintain Buddhism as a state religion.)[234]

Buddhism and the Caste System

Throughout history, Buddhism flourished among the lower classes of society.[235] A significant problem with Hinduism is that it is based on and promotes the social caste system.[236] As such, if one is born into a low caste, one will always be there, even upon reincarnation. That can be very depressing. Gautama rejected the caste system's assumption that a person's aptitudes were hereditary.[237] There are a few ways to escape the caste system while remaining in India. First, one can join the military or become a monk or ascetic. However, one could also convert to Buddhism, Christianity, Islam, Jainism, or Sikhism, among other religions, that do not recognize the caste system.[238]

Buddhism as a Religion

As we discussed earlier, most people believe a religion requires at minimum a belief in a deity (or deities) and a canonized holy text (or texts). Earlier, we reviewed a number of sacred texts believed to be holy by either the *Theravada* or *Mahayana* traditions. As for a deity, Buddhists deny the existence of any omnipotent or omniscient deity that does not decay and die.[239] Gautama insisted he was merely a mortal human being. In *Thera-*

---

234. Bechert, Gombrich, eds., *The World of Buddhism*, 116.

235. Bechert, Gombrich, eds., *The World of Buddhism*, 10.

236. *Bhagavad Vita* (a sacred text for Hinduism written during the lifetime of Buddha) discussed the caste system. (Lehr, *Militant Buddhism*, 49)

237. Smith, *The World's Religions*, 98.

238. Bechert and Gombrich, eds., *The World of Buddhism*, 12.

239. Lehr, *Militant Buddhism*, 16.

vada Buddhism, Buddha is venerated as the teacher who showed the way but not worshipped as a god or deity.[240]

However, according to some sacred texts, a Buddha is far more than that. According to the *Lotus Sutra*, Buddhas are the most honored of humans, to whom kings bowed at their feet, to whom all human beings should pay homage, and with the ability to send rays of light to reveal the ultimate reality of things. In fact, the *Sutra* claims that no one can fully know the powers of a Buddha.[241] As such, perhaps a Buddha could be a "human deity," which is how Christianity came to perceive Jesus Christ. Smith posed a reverse logic in that if Buddhism is recognized as a world religion, then perhaps religions do not require belief in a deity or god.[242]

Now that we have completed a brief review of Buddhism, a global religion, it is time to discuss how it facilitates violence and conflict.

---

240. Lehr, *Militant Buddhism*, 15.

241. Shinozaki, Ziporyn, and Earhart, translators, *The Threefold Lotus Sutra*, 37, 51, 56, 58, 295.

242. Smith, *The World's Religions*, 114.

CHAPTER 6

Buddhism and Conflict

RELIGIONS AROUND THE WORLD often have reputations. Islam has a widespread reputation of being one of the world's most violent religions. Buddhism, on the other hand, has the reputation of being one of the most peaceful religions in the world.[1] Its doctrine of *ahisma* (i.e., non-violence) is one of the fundamental tenets of Buddhism found in the *Tripitaka*. This serves as a stand against acts of violence by Buddhists.[2] So, where Islam was spread primarily by the sword, Buddhism was spread by traders and missionaries—not by force.[3] Despite this common perception, violence has been part of Buddhism for over 2,500 years. In fact, Nicholas Gier, a professor of philosophy at the University of Idaho, noted when reflecting on Buddhism (which primarily resides in Asia), "Buddhism is the religion with the worst violence record in Asia."[4]

All religions accommodate violence and conflict to some degree.[5] Regarding Buddhism, Michael Jerryson, a professor of religious studies at Eckerd College, Florida, found that its "mythohistories" justified violence; these histories are rife with tales of warfare, discussed previously.[6] Even though Buddha specifically directed his followers to spread the *dharma* peacefully, Peter Lehr, a lecturer on terrorism studies at the University of

---

1. Keyes, "Theravada Buddhism and Buddhist Nationalism: Sri Lanka, Myanmar, Cambodia, and Thailand," 41.
2. Lehr, *Militant Buddhism*, 2, 45.
3. Parrinder, *World Religions*, 303.
4. Gier, *The Origins of Religious Violence*, xiii.
5. Jerryson and Juergensmeyer, eds., *Buddhist Warfare*, 184.
6. Jerryson and Juergensmeyer, eds., *Buddhist Warfare*, 7.

Saint Andrews, and Jerryson determined that Buddhist battles occurred due to ideological differences between Buddhist traditions and when spreading Buddhist beliefs.[7]

Using Japan as an example of the various Buddhist internal battles, during its Heian Period (950-1185 CE), Xue Yu, a professor at the Chinese University in Hong Kong, noted that, "Monks were trained and employed to invade other's temples or protect their own from invasion."[8] As such, some Buddhist temples of the Tendai tradition established groups of warrior monks called *Sohei*. These groups fought one another for political influence, to protect land, and to intimidate rival traditions of Buddhism.[9] From 1336 to 1573 CE, during the "warring states era" in Japan, militant Buddhist leagues rose in revolt against Samurai landlords *and one another*. During this era of widespread warfare, many Buddhist temples and monasteries were destroyed. Jerryson concluded that "The military has been involved with Buddhist affairs throughout the history of Buddhism."[10]

Turning to Buddhist sacred texts and the Buddhist primary traditions, we find justification to use violence and participate in conflict.[11] Jerryson observed that "Buddhist traditions have a long and rich history of alternate interpretations and translations of texts that address violence...."[12] In both the primary Buddhist traditions, *Mahayana* and *Theravada*, there are differences regarding the justification for violence. *Theravada* Buddhism, the more conservative tradition, only allows for violence in defense of Buddhism—not its expansion.[13] Yu explained that "In the Pali canon, Buddha did not declare offensive war to be immoral nor did he directly condemn military leaders who would initiate such war. He merely stated that the attack would not be successful."[14] As such, *Theravada* Buddhism contains elements of *just war* in it.[15]

---

7. Lehr, *Militant Buddhism*, 36; Jerryson and Juergensmeyer, eds., *Buddhist Warfare*, 8.

8. Tikhonov and Brekke, eds., *Buddhism and Violence*, 202.

9. Snelling, *The Buddhist Handbook*, 178.

10. Jerryson and Juergensmeyer, eds., *Buddhist Warfare*, 180.

11. Lehr, *Militant Buddhism*, 195.

12. Jerryson, *Buddhist Fury*, 17.

13. Lehr, *Militant Buddhism*, 45; https://theconversation.com/militant-buddhism-is-on-the-march-in-south-east-asia-where-did-it-come-from-86632

14. Tikhonov and Brekke, eds., *Buddhism and Violence*, 195.

15. Lehr, *Militant Buddhism*, 47.

However, the *Mahayana* tradition justifies using violence to either eliminate conflict or to save another person's life, though the Buddhists performing the violent act must not have any ill thoughts or intentions to accommodate karma.[16] The killing must be an act of charity whereby the ends justify the means.[17] For example, killing one person to prevent that person from killing others is justified. Yu noted that "Monks may kill evil ones if such an act of killing is aimed as saving more lives or safeguarding the *dharma*."[18] Eugene Ford, a lecturer at the Sciences Po Collège Universitaire de Reims, also found this to be valid for the *Mahayana* tradition practiced in Japan, writing that, "It is good to kill evil. Japanese Buddhists are justified to fight with an evil enemy."[19]

In the case of *bodhisattvas* (Buddhas-to-Be), it is their duty to commit the sin of killing to prevent non-*bodhisattvas* from having to sin. In other words, it is better to sin than to let others sin.[20] Buddha taught that one must sacrifice the lesser good for the greater good. So, where the act of killing is certainly demeritorious, the merit earned can be greater.[21]

Throughout history, it is when religions become integrated with governing polities that conflict becomes more likely. Vladimir Tikhonov, a professor at the University of Oslo, found that "Buddhism has been a powerful force in the political arena since its beginning."[22] Walpola Rahula Thero, a Sri Lankan Buddhist monk and a professor of history and religion at Northwestern University, declared that "According to Buddhism, politics is a righteous deed. Politics is connected with life. So is religion. The two can never be separated."[23] Nicholas Gier, a professor of philosophy at the University of Idaho, wrote that "whenever religious and national identities are fused, one will find religiously-motivated violence."[24] Charles Keyes, a professor of Buddhist Studies at the University of Washington, determined

---

16. Tikhonov and Brekke, eds., *Buddhism and Violence*, 195; Jerryson and Jeurgensmeyer, eds., *Buddhist Warfare*, 47, 9.
17. Jerryson and Jeurgensmeyer, eds., *Buddhist Warfare*, 44.
18. Tikhonov and Brekke, eds., *Buddhism and Violence*, 197.
19. Eugene Ford, *Cold War Monks*, 16.
20. Jerryson and Jeurgensmeyer, eds., *Buddhist Warfare*, 41, 42.
21. Tikhonov and Brekke, eds., *Buddhism and Violence*, 183.
22. Tikhonov and Brekke, eds., *Buddhism and Violence*, 4.
23. Thero, *The Heritage of Bhikkhu*, 122–123.
24. Gier, *The Origins of Religious Violence*, 252.

that "Violence justified by religion became common in Buddhism once it became affiliated with state governments."[25]

The standard practice was for states to adopt Buddhism as their official religion in return for Buddhist justification for states to use violence.[26] Once a religion co-exists with a state, an attack on one was perceived as an attack on both.[27] Using a current case, Kaushik Roy, a professor of history at the Jadavpur University in Calcutta, India, noted that an attack by Muslims on a Buddhist temple or monastery would be considered an attack on not only Buddhism, but all of Thailand as well.[28] Moreover, Buddhist states use violence both externally (against other states, kingdoms, or religions) as well as internally (against dissidents.)[29] Buddhism allows for violence in defense of the religion, in defense of a country with Buddhism as its official religion, or the protection of innocent lives.[30] It allows kings the right to rule and to enforce this rule using violence.[31] Buddhist kings will incur little sin or lose many merits if people are killed in a war he tried to prevent. In fact, such a *just war* may instead generate great merit for the ruler.[32] On the other hand, according to Jerryson, "Buddhist kings have a disturbing tendency for mass violence against non-Buddhists."[33] As well, Buddhist kings also waged offensive war against other Buddhist kings, notably in Southeast Asia.[34] One reason this was legitimized within Buddhism is that offensive combat was equated to preventive war, meaning it is acceptable to attack an enemy before an attack by the enemy.[35]

Buddhists have engaged in war since the 3rd century BCE.[36] Kings throughout northeastern and southeastern Asia frequently enlisted

---

25. Keyes, "Theravada Buddhism and Buddhist Nationalism: Sri Lanka, Myanmar, Cambodia, and Thailand," 41; Jerryson and Juergensmeyer, eds., *Buddhist Warfare*, 38.
26. Jerryson and Juergensmeyer, eds., *Buddhist Warfare*, 13.
27. Jerryson and Juergensmeyer, eds., *Buddhist Warfare*, 38.
28. Roy, *Hinduism and the Ethics of Warfare in South Asia*, 41.
29. Jerryson and Juergensmeyer, eds., *Buddhist Warfare*, 38.
30. Tikhonov and Brekke, eds., *Buddhism and Violence*, 198.
31. Jerryson and Juergensmeyer, eds., *Buddhist Warfare*, 13.
32. Tikhonov and Brekke, eds., *Buddhism and Violence*, 201.
33. Jerryson and Juergensmeyer, eds., *Buddhist Warfare*, 63.
34. Tikhonov and Brekke, eds., *Buddhism and Violence*, 202.
35. Jerryson and Juergensmeyer, eds., *Buddhist Warfare*, 39.
36. Jerryson and Juergensmeyer, eds., *Buddhist Warfare*, 59.

Buddhist monks to fight on their behalf.[37] In China, Buddhist monks were famous for going to war to serve the homeland. For example, they went to war against Japanese pirates in the 15th and 16th centuries.[38] Korean kings enlisted their own Buddhist armies to fight against foreign invaders. Monks have been enlisted by the thousands over the centuries.[39] In Japan, Buddhist military groups became an institution in society.[40] In Thailand, kings passed all military responsibilities to the Thai Buddhist *Sangha*.[41] The logical consequence of this merging of state and religion is that: 1) there are such things as military monks (usually kept secret), and 2) monks are involved in violence.[42] After all, as the Buddhist monk Sumedhananda prophesized, "If a man dies, it is acceptable. But, if a race or religion dies, you can never get it back."[43]

As previously discussed, monks live and operate out of monasteries. Counter-intuitively, monasteries often housed law enforcement and military personnel. They even became military outposts and military headquarters.[44] For example, in Tibet, each monastery had its own private army as the various Tibetan Buddhist sects fought against one another over the centuries (all while living in harmony with Muslims!).[45] In Nepal, it was common for monasteries to have armories so that their monks could fight in both sectarian and non-sectarian battles.[46] Finally, monasteries were also places of refuge for terrorized civilians. Therefore, it was beneficial to have armed, military monks protecting the religion, temples, monasteries, other monks, and Buddhist laypeople.[47] As Lehr wrote, "An armed monk is better than no monk at all."[48]

---

37. Jerryson and Juergensmeyer, eds., *Buddhist Warfare*, 30–33.
38. Jerryson and Juergensmeyer, eds., *Buddhist Warfare*, 31.
39. Jerryson and Juergensmeyer, eds., *Buddhist Warfare*, 33.
40. Jerryson and Juergensmeyer, eds., *Buddhist Warfare*, 33.
41. Jerryson and Juergensmeyer, eds., *Buddhist Warfare*, 180.
42. Jerryson, *Buddhist Fury*, 16.
43. Beech, "Buddhists Go to Battle: When Nationalism Overrides Pacifism," https://www.nytimes.com/2019/07/08/world/asia/buddhism-militant-rise.html
44. Jerryson and Juergensmeyer, eds., *Buddhist Warfare*, 37.
45. Gier, *The Origins of Religious Violence*, 129, 133.
46. Gier, *The Origins of Religious Violence*, 165.
47. Lehr, *Militant Buddhism*, 222.
48. Lehr, *Militant Buddhism*, 221.

As it turns out, all national Buddhist traditions have had military monks,[49] including those found in China, Japan, Korea, Thailand, and Sri Lanka.[50] Suwanna Satha-Anand, a professor of Buddhist philosophy at Chulalongkorn University in Bangkok, Thailand, explained, "It is clear that nationalism and patriotism are put at the highest level thus justifying the violation of the first Buddhist precept."[51] Buddhist military monks are justified in killing if their *intention* is to protect either Buddhism itself or the nation that has embraced it.[52] And, lest there be any doubt, Buddhist monks were usually among the best soldiers in a country's military forces. According to Jerryson, "Monks were awarded military titles. This leaves us with little doubt as to their abilities as soldiers."[53]

Let us focus briefly on Japan as an example of Buddhism and conflict. In Japan, Buddhist doctrines legitimize both killing and dying in combat.[54] Lehr explained, "The history of Japanese Buddhism saw a militant spirit among the *Sangha* from the Middle Ages. Monks were trained and employed to invade other's temples or protect their own from invasion."[55] In this part of the world, *Mahayana* Buddhism advocates taking a sword to demons as it is perceived as good to kill evil and preserve the true *dharma*.[56] In other words, it believes in the humane killing of one person so that many may live, as long as the killer has pure intentions.[57] Regarding war, Buddhism did not see it as either inherently good or bad.[58]

One of the Japanese Buddhist traditions is Zen Buddhism, consisting of three primary sects – Rinzai, Soto, and Obaku. One could make the cases that Rinzai Zen was preferred by the Shogun; Soto Zen by peasants; and Obaku Zen by Chinese merchants in Japan. In the first half of the 20th century, Rinzai Zen became the religion of the Samurai class, facilitating

---

49. Lehr, *Militant Buddhism*, 221.
50. Jerryson and Juergensmeyer, eds., *Buddhist Warfare*, 60.
51. Tikhonov and Brekke, eds., *Buddhism and Violence*, 183.
52. Lehr, *Militant Buddhism*, 2; Tikhonov and Brekke, eds., *Buddhism and Violence*, 184.
53. Jerryson and Juergensmeyer, eds., *Buddhist Warfare*, 28.
54. Lehr, *Militant Buddhism*, 154.
55. Lehr, *Militant Buddhism*, 202.
56. Ford, *Cold War Monks*, 16, 17; Victoria, *Zen at War*, 92.
57. Victoria, *Zen at War*, 87.
58. Victoria, *Zen at War*, 88.

warrior training, including learning and following *Bushido*.⁵⁹ Lin-ji, Yixuan, a Zen Master, encouraged his followers to free themselves of worldly constraints. He famously advocated,

> Followers of the Way, if you want to get the kind of understanding that accords with the *Dharma*, never be misled by others. Whether you're facing inward or facing outward, whatever you meet up with, just kill it! If you meet a Buddha, kill the Buddha. If you meet a patriarch, kill the patriarch. If you meet an arhat, kill the arhat. If you meet your parents, kill your parents. If you meet your kinfolk, kill your kinfolk. Then for the first time you will gain emancipation, will not be entangled with things, will pass freely anywhere you wish to go.⁶⁰

This militarization of Buddhism led Japan to kill millions of people in Asian countries, allegedly to save the native Asians from becoming slaves of the Westerners.⁶¹

Zen Buddhism is a form of Chinese *Mahayana* Buddhism introduced to Japan by Priest Eisai from China at the beginning of the Kamakura period (1135-1333 CE).⁶² To most people, Zen Buddhism is about discovering one's inner serenity and social peace. However, in the 1930s and 1940s, Zen was hijacked by the Hirohito regime to support the war effort.

To many Americans, Zen Buddhists primarily devote themselves to discovering inner serenity and social peace. However, during World War II, with the active support of Zen Buddhism, Japan controlled Manchuria, Korea, Vietnam, Burma, Thailand, Malaysia, Indonesia, Philippines, and parts of the Russian Maritime Province (see map of Imperial Japan in 1942). From 1937 until the end of World War II in 1945, Japan had killed over ten million people, including almost six million Chinese, Indonesians, Koreans, Filipinos, and Vietnamese, among others.⁶³ Years after the War, Zen leaders began to express remorse for Zen's enabling of Imperial Japan.

59. Lehr, *Militant Buddhism*, 203.

60. *Lin-Chi Lu*, translation from Burton Watson, *The Zen Teachings of Master Lin-Chi*, 52.

61. *Lin-Chi Lu*, translation from Burton Watson, *The Zen Teachings of Master Lin-Chi Lu*, 203. (Much like the American forces burning villages in the Vietnam Conflict to save them from communism.)

62. Victoria, *Zen at War*, 99.

63. Rummel, *Statistics of Democide*, https://www.hawaii.edu/powerkills/SOD.CHAP3.HTM#:~:text=From%20the%20invasion%20of%20China,including%20Western%20prisoners%20of%20war

According to Allan Jalon, a professor of journalism at Columbia University, "the leaders of one of the largest denominations in Japan remorsefully compared their former religious fanaticism during Japan's brutal expansionism in the 1930's and 1940's to today's murderously militant Islamists."[64] While Japan's surrender in 1945 marked an end to Imperial Zen Buddhism and State Shinto, Zen's connection to the Japanese military has not disappeared.[65] In fact, Victoria observed that "There is no guarantee that Zen's future, whether in the East or West, will not once again include support for the mass destruction of human life that is modern warfare."[66]

Daisetsu Suzuki (1870-1966) was a well-known Japanese scholar and author of many books on Zen Buddhism and Shinto who followed Rinzai Zen Buddhism. He wrote that "Religion and the state must necessarily support each other if they are to achieve wholeness. Religion should seek to preserve the existence of the state."[67] He said that Japan has the right to pursue its commercial and trade ambitions as it sees fit and that those who interfere should be punished with the support of Japan's religions.[68] In his assessment of the first half of the 20th century (i.e., State Shinto and Zen Buddhism), Suzuki considered Shinto a primitive religion and blamed it for Japan's militaristic past instead of Zen Buddhism.[69] He called for a renewal of Japanese Zen after laying blame for its corruption during this period on Zen priests and their establishment.[70]

---

64. Jalon, "Meditating On War And Guilt, Zen Says It's Sorry," https://www.nytimes.com/2003/01/11/books/meditating-on-war-and-guilt-zen-says-it-s-sorry.html

65. Victoria, *Zen at War*, 147, 190.

66. Victoria, *Zen at War*, xi.

67. Victoria, *Zen at War*, 23.

68. Victoria, *Zen at War*, 25.

69. Victoria, *Zen at War*, 150.

70. Victoria, *Zen at War*, 148.

KILLING FOR RELIGION

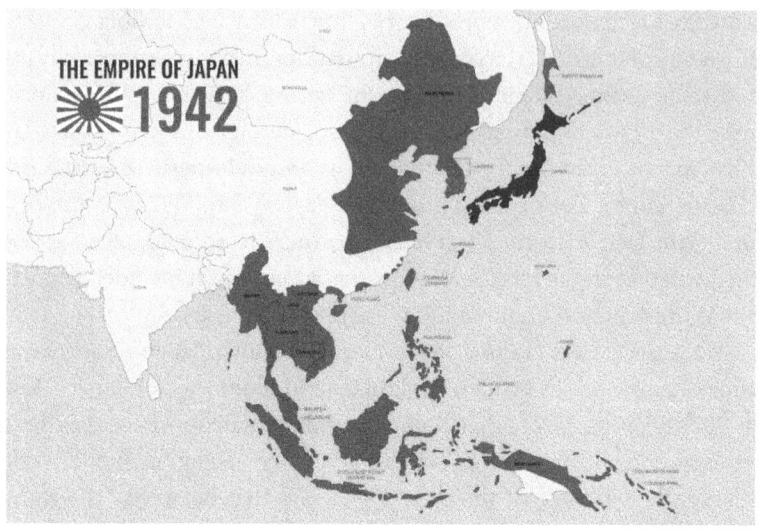

Empire of Japan 1942[71]

Finally, Buddhism played an instrumental part in overthrowing European colonialism in Southeast Asia (SEA). Except for Thailand, every SEA country saw its religious and monarchical institutions dismantled by colonial regimes.[72] Most of the religious violence in SEA came as a result of these colonial incursions into India, Sri Lanka, and Myanmar.[73] The primary imperial European country in Asia beginning in the 18th century was Great Britain. In Sri Lanka, Buddhist monks fought for national independence from British colonial rule.[74] When the British imperialists arrived, they used the *divide and conquer* approach to maintain control and stability over the people of the countries they occupied. However, as occurred everywhere this policy was implemented, it led to negative consequences that continue to linger today.[75] It should also be noted that until the British arrived, Buddhists and Muslims lived in relative peace together throughout SEA, notably in Myanmar (where Muslims outnumbered Buddhists).[76]

71. Shutterstock, https://www.shutterstock.com/image-vector/map-empire-japan japanese-during-wwii-1942-1840466548

72. Beech, "Buddhists Go to Battle: When Nationalism Overrides Pacifism," 108.

73. Gier, *The Origins of Religious Violence*, xi.

74. Tikhonov and Brekke, eds., *Buddhism and Violence*, 202.

75. Gier, *The Origins of Religious Violence*, 79.

76. Gier, *The Origins of Religious Violence*, 69.

Not only did Buddhist monks provide the inspiration and support for anti-colonial, nationalist movements, they also actively participated in the insurgencies. For example, in 1930, Buddhist monks killed four Europeans in Rangoon.[77]

With this background on how and why Buddhists justified becoming violent, let us review how and where Buddhism is involved in conflict in Asia today, including (in the following order) South Korea, Thailand, Myanmar, Cambodia, and Laos (see map of Southeast Asia). I will conclude this chapter with a discussion of Buddhist conflict regarding Islam.

South Korea

Shortly after World War II ended in 1945, the Korean War began (in 1950). Syngman Rhee (a Methodist) became South Korea's first president and ruled as a dictator from 1948-1960. He worked against the Korean Buddhists by associating them with Japan. A major philosophical rift within the Korean *Sangha* erupted over whether monks could be married (the Japanese Buddhist custom) or remain celibate (the Korean Buddhist custom). Riots occurred at many Buddhist temples over this issue, which lessened the appeal of Buddhism in South Korea (much to the delight of Christian missionaries who were making significant inroads into Asia at this time). During the Korean War, the Korean Jogye Order provided justification for China to enter the conflict in the 1950s, supporting North Korea.[78]

Thailand

During the 1960s, communism was on the march throughout Southeast Asia. Due to the British colonial rule for well over a century, Buddhist monks had become politically active for independence in Thailand, Burma, Laos, Cambodia, Sri Lanka, and Vietnam.[79] In Thailand, a right-wing monk named Kittivudho fused Buddhism with anti-communism. He promoted Buddhism as an alternative to communism and imperialism.[80] He went so far as to proclaim that killing communists was *not* a sin and that

77. Tikhonov and Brekke, eds., *Buddhism and Violence*, 4;
78. Jerryson and Juergensmeyer, eds., *Buddhist Warfare*, 14.
79. Jerryson and Juergensmeyer, eds., *Buddhist Warfare*, 5.
80. Ford, *Cold War Monks*, 31.

communist-leaning movements in Thailand should be violently repressed.[81] He even offered his monastery to vigilante groups to fight communists.[82]

Myanmar (Burma)

To begin, the British fought three wars against Burma before conquering it in 1885.[83] Britain ruled Burma as it did the rest of its empire by dividing the population against itself based on ethnicity, religion, or language – among other categories.[84] After World War II, in 1948, Burma became an independent country. In 1960, Buddhism became the state religion.[85] In 1989, Burma changed its name to Myanmar.

Nearly 90 percent of the fifty-two million citizens of Myanmar follow *Theravada* Buddhism. Today, Myanmar is the center of one of the largest refugee crises in the world. The Government of Myanmar, with the full support of the Buddhist *Sangha*, has forcibly displaced hundreds of thousands of Rohingya Muslims living in the southwestern part of the country in the province of Rakhine – the regional interface between Buddhist and Muslim Asia.[86] In 2020, there were approximately one million Rohingya citizens in Myanmar. Though the Myanmar government considers them illegal immigrants, they trace their origins in the region to the 15th century CE.[87]

---

81. Ford, *Cold War Monks*, 11.
82. Ford, *Cold War Monks*, 11.
83. Von de Waals, *The Rohingya in Myanmar*, 11.
84. Von de Waals, *The Rohingya in Myanmar*, 11.
85. Von de Waals, *The Rohingya in Myanmar*, 12, 13.
86. Von de Waals, *The Rohingya in Myanmar*, 15.
87. https://www.worldvision.org/refugees-news-stories/rohingya-refugees-bangladesh-facts#:~:text=The%20Rohingya%20people%20are%20a,which%20borders%20Bangladesh%20and%20India.

Buddhism and Conflict

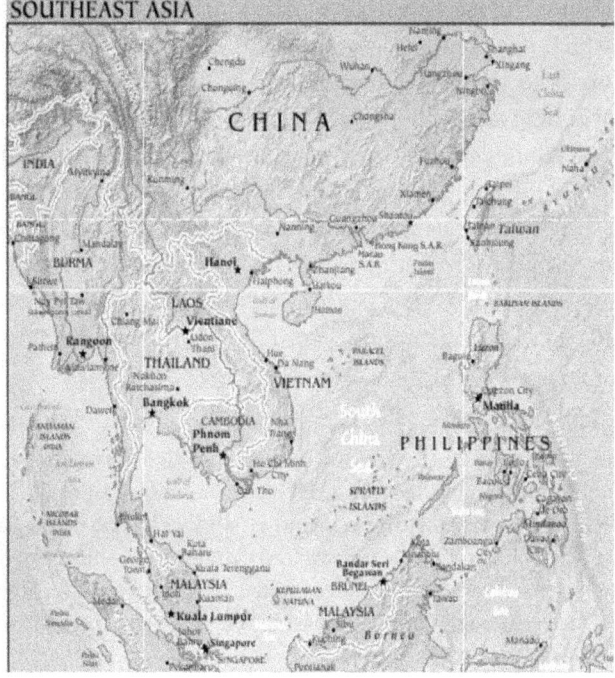

Map of Southeast Asia[88]

An example of the extreme measures implemented by the government against its Muslim citizens, Myanmar passed the Population Control Act to limit the number of children in Muslim areas to just two (an act of genocide according to the United Nations).[89] Other restrictions on these Muslims include marriage, family planning, employment, education, and freedom of movement.[90] Ashin Wirathu, a Burmese Buddhist nationalist monk, is the leader of the 969 Movement in Myanmar, which opposes Islam's expansion in the country. Social media giant Facebook banned his webpage on the charge of spreading religious hatred towards Islam. In 2013, *Time* magazine featured him on its cover as "The Face of Buddhist Terror." Wirathu even claimed his Muslim opponents call him the "Burmese Bin Laden."[91]

88. CIA World Factbook, http://apeda.in/agriexchange/maps/refmap_southeast_asia.html

89. Von de Waals, *The Rohingya in Myanmar*, 15.

90. Albert and Maizland, "The Rohingya Crisis," https://www.cfr.org/backgrounder/rohingya-crisis

91. https://www.theguardian.com/world/2019/may/29/myanmar-police-hunt

The Rohingyas have been forced to flee primarily to neighboring Bangladesh, which does not have the capacity to care for them, and to other SEA countries to the south (usually by sea). Beginning in 2017, a mass exodus of Rohingya people began once Myanmar's security forces began slaughtering them, claiming they were just trying to reinstate stability in Rakhine. Over the past decade, several hundred Rohingya have been murdered, and their mosques and homes have been destroyed. As well, their citizenship has been revoked, so they are now illegal immigrants in their own country. Even the United Nations accused the Myanmar government of executing genocide operations against the Rohingya people.[92] According to Lehr,

> Buddhist blood is boiling in Burma, also known as Myanmar--and plenty of Muslim blood is being spilled. Over the past year, Buddhist mobs have targeted members of the minority faith, and incendiary rhetoric from Wirathu--he goes by one name--and other hard-line monks is fanning the flames of religious chauvinism. Scores of Muslims have been killed, according to government statistics, although international human-rights workers put the number in the hundreds.[93]

Cambodia

Turning to Cambodia, in the 1970s, the communist Khmer Rouge under Pol Pot rooted out and destroyed the Cambodian *Sangha* and Buddhist temples in its effort to remake the country. For over six centuries, Buddhism was the primary religion in Cambodia, with temple monasteries in almost every community in the country. However, as Buddhism came up against the growing communist movements in Asia, it faced disaster in Cambodia.[94] Keyes wrote,

> During the war between 1970 and 1975 more than one-third of the [4,000] monasteries were destroyed; many [of the 65,000] monks and novices were killed, left the order, or became refugees. An estimate made in 1980 showed that five out of every eight monks had been executed during the Pol Pot regime; those monks

---

-buddhist-bin-laden-over-suu-kyi-comments

92. Von de Waals, *The Rohingya in Myanmar*, 20.
93. Lehr, *Militant Buddhism*, 35.
94. Ford, *Cold War Monks*, 238.

and novices who were not killed were forced to disrobe. Temple-monasteries were turned into storage centers, prisons, even extermination camps.[95]

Laos

In late 1975, Laos fell to the Vietnamese communists. The communists quickly abolished the monarchy, removed as much French influence in the country as possible, and then co-opted Buddhism.[96] The religion was modified to align with communist principles. The Buddhism taught in Laos was far more "Marxist" than what was practiced by the people. For example, *Nirvana* was no longer the goal to escape the endless cycle of rebirth. Instead, when people die, they become one with the earth.[97] Buddhist monks taught both Marxist-Leninism as well as Buddhism. Moreover, Buddha was held in the same esteem as Marx and Lenin. Buddhism was praised at the pagodas, while communism was taught at mandatory political meetings. Hence, pagodas were used for both political seminars and prayer services. Revolutionary songs were composed to replace rock-and-roll music, and young people were asked not to wear Western attire, such as blue jeans.[98] Even the Laos Buddhist Institute ended up being run by communists. The Laotian government was using the most authoritative voice in the country—Buddhist monks—to bring communism to the people. In this way, communist leaders made the same arrangement that kings had made centuries earlier; the Laos Buddhist *Sangha* would provide legitimacy for the rulers in return for state support. As such, there was no conflict involving Buddhism in Laos.

---

95. Keyes, "Theravada Buddhism and Buddhist Nationalism: Sri Lanka, Myanmar, Cambodia, and Thailand," https://www.culturalsurvival.org/publications/cultural-survival-quarterly/buddhism-and-revolution-cambodia

96. Ford, *Cold War Monks*, 256; Becker, "Buddhism in Laos Adapts to Communist Tenets," https://www.washingtonpost.com/archive/politics/1979/05/08/buddhism-in-laos-adapts-to-communist-tenets/90a0fee0-cd99-4290-b688-6bdfb8945f72/

97. Becker, "Buddhism in Laos Adapts to Communist Tenets," https://www.washingtonpost.com/archive/politics/1979/05/08/buddhism-in-laos-adapts-to-communist-tenets/90a0fee0-cd99-4290-b688-6bdfb8945f72/

98. Becker, "Buddhism in Laos Adapts to Communist Tenets," https://www.washingtonpost.com/archive/politics/1979/05/08/buddhism-in-laos-adapts-to-communist-tenets/90a0fee0-cd99-4290-b688-6bdfb8945f72/

Islam

In Hinduism, the caste system has at the bottom a category called "Others" – primarily to identify foreigners. For Buddhists, Muslims are considered Others. As Lehr explained, "The 'othering' of Muslims is one of the current core themes or militant Buddhism. Muslims are constructed as the implacable enemies of Buddhism."[99] Buddhist rhetoric against Muslims is founded on the numerous worldwide terrorist attacks executed by Muslim terrorist groups, such as the al-Qaeda terrorist attack on the United States on September 11, 2001. Hannah Beech, the Southeast Asia Bureau Chief for the *New York Times*, concluded that "Buddhists have entered the era of militant tribalism, casting themselves as spiritual warriors who must defend their faith against an outside force."[100]

The conflict involving Buddhism today is focused primarily on Islam, going back many centuries. Islam began spreading throughout Asia between the 7th and 11th centuries. Often, the installation of Islam in a country or kingdom meant the forced removal of Buddhism.[101] Sri Lankan Abbot Ambalangoda declared, "Think of what used to be Buddhist lands: Afghanistan, Pakistan, Kashmir, Indonesia. They have all been *destroyed* by Islam."[102]

The concern is that Islam will continue expanding and replacing Buddhism in countries across Asia, eventually posing an existential threat to Buddhism itself.[103] The primary basis for this concern is demographic. Buddhism and Buddhists are projected to decline in the foreseeable future, while Islam and Muslims are projected to continue growing rapidly. Akhilesh Pillalamarri, an international relations analyst in India, provided the following analysis:

> Buddhism was arguably the world's largest religion a century ago, if one counts everyone who also followed Chinese folk religion, Shinto, and other East Asian religions. In the modern era, Buddhism has been particularly vulnerable, however, to both

---

99. Lehr, *Militant Buddhism*, 214, 232.

100. Beech, "Buddhists Go to Battle: When Nationalism Overrides Pacifism," https://www.nytimes.com/2019/07/08/world/asia/buddhism-militant-rise.html

101. https://thediplomat.com/2017/10/buddhism-and-islam-in-asia-a-long-and-complicated-history/

102. https://www.nytimes.com/2019/07/08/world/asia/buddhism-militant-rise.html

103. Gunasingham, "Buddhist Extremism in Sri Lanka and Myanmar: An Examination," 1.

secularism and evangelism from other religions. According to a Pew survey, alone among the world's major religions (including Christianity, Islam, Hinduism, and Chinese folk religion), Buddhism and its adherents are projected to decline both in terms of raw numbers, and as a percentage of the world population. The world Buddhist population is projected to fall from 488 million to 486 million people, and from 7 percent to 5 percent of total share. Christianity and Islam are still growing; in particular, the latter will grow from around 23 percent of the global population to 30 percent by 2050. Put another way, there will be six times as many Muslims as Buddhists by then.[104]

Today, *Theravada* Buddhists constitute the overwhelming majority in five Southeast Asian countries—Sri Lanka, Myanmar, Cambodia, Laos, and Thailand. In these countries, *Theravada* Buddhism has been intentionally distorted to justify violence in defense of Buddhism against the onslaught of Islam.[105] According to Mikael Gravers, an anthropologist at Aarhus University in Denmark, the senior monks that he interviewed recently told him that Buddhism and Buddhist states need to be defended *by any means*.[106] To make this happen, monks are recruited and trained to fight in defense of Buddhism and their respective countries. In 2013, Sri Lanka's Defense Secretary Gotabhaya Rajapaksa, the guest of honor at the opening of a Buddhist Brigade training school, referred to the trainee monks as those who "protect our country, religion, and race."[107]

Southeast Asia (SEA) countries are revising their constitutions to identify Buddhism as their national religion – such as in Sri Lanka in 1978.[108] Moreover, hardline Buddhist organizations have been formed in these countries as well, including the Bodu Bala Sena (BBS – Buddhist Power Force) in Sri Lanka and the Organization for the Protection of Race

---

104. Pillalamarri, "Buddhism and Islam in Asia: A Long and Complicated History," https://thediplomat.com/2017/10/buddhism-and-islam-in-asia-a-long-and-complicated-history/

105. Gunasingham, "Buddhist Extremism in Sri Lanka and Myanmar: An Examination," 1.

106. Beech, "Buddhists Go to Battle: When Nationalism Overrides Pacifism," https://www.nytimes.com/2019/07/08/world/asia/buddhism-militant-rise.html

107. Strathern, "Why are Buddhist Monks Attacking Muslims?" https://www.bbc.com/news/magazine-22356306

108. Gunasingham, "Buddhist Extremism in Sri Lanka and Myanmar: An Examination," 2.

and Religion (MaBa Tha in Myanmar).[109] These groups propagate myths to incite violence against Muslims.[110]

While Buddhists prefer to remain peaceful and humble servants to their communities, the continued growth in adherents and militant expansion of Islam over the centuries has changed the general perception of Buddhism. Buddhism is currently in a fight for its very existence against Islam around the world. This conflict entails both mental and physical capacities. Islam also threatens Christianity, but not necessarily Shinto – the topic of the following two chapters.

---

109. Gunasingham, "Buddhist Extremism in Sri Lanka and Myanmar: An Examination," 1.

110. Gunasingham, "Buddhist Extremism in Sri Lanka and Myanmar: An Examination," 3.

CHAPTER 7

Shinto

As HINDUISM IS TO India, Shinto is to Japan. Both are ancient indigenous religions that dominate their respective countries.

Background

In ancient times in Japan, religion was inseparable from daily life.[1] The religion in the earliest times was Shinto. Shinto is the oldest indigenous religion in Japan with elements of it dating back to the 7th century BCE.[2] (However, the rituals and practices performed today appear to have been standardized around the 7th century CE.) The word "Shinto" comes from the Chinese words *shen* (gods) and *tao* (way); hence, "the way of gods."[3] Shinto is about keeping the human soul in harmony with nature and with the spirits of the natural world. Japanese people say it is impossible to understand Japan without understanding Shinto.[4]

---

1. Nelson, *A Year in the Life of a Shinto Shrine*, 9.

2. Langley, *World Religions*, 44; Parrinder, *World Religions*, 353. It had much in common with the Shamanism being practiced in Northeast Asia at that time.

3. Barton, "Buddhism and Shinto: The Two Pillars of Japanese Culture," https://japanology.org/2016/06/buddhism-and-shinto-the-two-pillars-of-japanese-culture/#:~:text=Japan%20is%20home%20to%20not,with%20virtually%20the%20same%20breath; Langley, 45; Kami is both singular and plural in the Japanese language.

4. Mason, *The Meaning of Shinto*, 15.

Kami

The Japanese phrase for spirit, god, honor, and respect is *Kami-no-Michi* (the "Way of Kami").[5] *Kami* is a Shinto expression meaning "divine spirit."[6] Hence, *kami* is the Japanese recognition of a *spiritual power* within the environment. The practitioners of Shinto hold that anything we can see or sense constitutes *kami*.[7] As such, *kami* resides in everything from people, temples, shrines, animals, plants, trees, rocks, wind, rain, lightning, to oceans. It signifies gods, spirits, mortals, ancestors, natural phenomena, and supernatural powers. In early Shinto, followers worshipped and prayed to objects of nature representing many millions of *kami*.[8]

The principal worship of *kami* is done at one of the more than eighty thousand public shrines in Japan (buildings constructed to function as a conduit for *kami*). Note that the objects of worship representing *kami* are similar for all sects of Shinto.[9] Shinto uses neither the statues nor paintings common in the Abrahamic religions to represent the divine spirit or Heaven in its shrines.[10] The typical representations of *kami* in Shinto shrines include either a jewel, sword, or mirror (the most common artifact).[11] In addition to animistic aspects, Shinto is a polytheistic religion which recognizes that there are millions of *kami* that deserve respect, worship, and supplication.[12]

Definition

Western definitions of religion are of limited relevance to Japan as the hallmarks of a Western religions do not really apply. Unlike most religions, Shinto has no absolutes, no moral code, no ethics, no organization, no leader, no founder, no philosophical schools of thought, no body of

---

5. Parrinder, *World Religions*, 354.
6. Mason, *The Meaning of Shinto*, 42.
7. Nelson, *A Year in the Life of a Shinto Shrine*, 27.
8. De Bary, ed., *Sources of Japanese Tradition Volume I*, 42.
9. De Bary, ed., *Sources of Japanese Tradition Volume I*, 21.
10. Mason, *The Meaning of Shinto*, 37.
11. Parrinder, *World Religions*, 356, 363; De Bary, ed., *Sources of Japanese Tradition Volume I*, 42. The three Sacred Treasures of Japan, are said to include a mirror called *Yata no Kagami* (representing the virtue of wisdom), a sword called *Kusanagi* (representing valor), and a jewel, *Yasakani no Magatama* (representing benevolence).
12. Barton "Buddhism and Shinto: The Two Pillars of Japanese Culture."

literature, no sacred texts like the Bible or *Qur'an*, and no belief in an afterlife.[13] According to JWT Mason, an American journalist and Shinto scholar, "In Shinto, there is no separation between the universe and divine creative spirit."[14] Another significant difference between the Abrahamic religions and Shinto is that Shinto does not perceive humanity as "sinful;" only needing guidance from *kami* to be in harmony with the world.[15]

Shinto has always been highly localized. Shrine and temple administrators traditionally did not coordinate activities with one another, even within the same village or town. They operated mostly independently, to include when and to which *kami* to celebrate. In fact, until 1868, Shinto knew no comprehensive organizational structure.[16]

One need not declare oneself as an adherent or practitioner of Shinto, as the religion is non-exclusive and has no rites of initiation *per se*. Anyone, including non-Japanese people, can arrive at a Shinto shrine, and, if they do the ritual practices and participate in the ceremonies according to custom, can be a part of the Shinto tradition. Tanaka, a Shinto priest of Kyoto, explained it as follows:

> In comparison to Western religions, such as Christianity, for which people believe in an absolute God, followers of Shinto sense *kehai* (presence of spirits) in the nature. Shinto never had holy scriptures like the Bible to follow, nor does it have a doctrine. It's more of a way of living, or the wisdom of how to live in harmony with the nature, while being grateful and respectful of all the spirits of life. Shinto has permeated everyday life in such a way that most people are not particularly conscious of its influence.[17]

---

13. Davies, *Japanese Culture*, 40–41; De Bary, ed., *Sources of Japanese Tradition Volume I*, 41; Barton, "Buddhism and Shinto: The Two Pillars of Japanese Culture," Hardacre, *Shinto and the State, 1868-1988*, xiv.

14. Mason, *The Meaning of Shinto*, 38.

15. Barton, "Buddhism and Shinto: The Two Pillars of Japanese Culture," https://japanology.org/2016/06/buddhism-and-shinto-the-two-pillars-of-japanese-culture/#:~:text=Japan%20is%20home%20to%20not,with%20virtually%20the%20same%20breath

16. Hardacre, *Shinto and the State, 1868-1988*, 10.

17. Tamashige, "Seeing Where Shinto and Buddhism Cross," https://www.japantimes.co.jp/culture/2013/05/16/arts/seeing-where-shinto-and-buddhism-cross/

Purification and Prayer

The most common Shinto rituals are those involving purification, including prayers.[18] When humans are out of harmony with nature, they accumulate impurities in the form of *tsumi* and *kegare*, which are terms that mean impurity, pollution, and diminution of life force. Thus, many Shinto practices are dedicated to purification. The Shinto purification ceremony assists the mind in getting rid of this waste.[19] However, Shinto purification ceremonies do not relieve an offender from responsibility for an impure action – they do not eliminate the obligation to make amends.[20]

Purification occurs in a number of ways even before the formal Shinto ceremony begins. One purifies via symbolic cleansing (*temizu*) of one's hands and mouth, usually involving water, before entering a shrine. Then, there is a preliminary purification ritual at the beginning of the ceremony using a wooden purification wand (*haraegushi*). Then, within the ceremony itself, there is usually the great prayer (*norito*) of purification.

As for prayer, Japanese people visited Shinto shrines to give thanks and pray for abundant crops and personal well-being.[21] For any new year, they pray for a good beginning.[22] According to the ancient and sacred text *Kojiki* (to be discussed soon), earthly and heavenly sins are to be exorcised and prayers are intended for *this* reality.[23] There usually are two acts of worship at any Shinto shrine: attending a shrine's ceremonies and giving of offerings (to include money).[24]

Today, there are around eighty thousand Shinto shrines and one hundred and fifty thousand Shinto priests in Japan to offer prayers or to celebrate festivals (*not* to provide religious instruction or guidance). Shinto shrines usually face south, but occasionally to the east (for luck).[25] It is estimated that over one hundred million (or around 80 percent) of the Japanese people are followers of Shinto. There are approximately three

---

18. De Bary, ed., *Sources of Japanese Tradition Volume I*, 41.
19. Mason, *The Meaning of Shinto*, 71.
20. Mason, *The Meaning of Shinto*, 97.
21. Hardacre, *Shinto and the State, 1868-1988*, 16; Nelson, *A Year in the Life of a Shinto Shrine*, 4.
22. Nelson, *A Year in the Life of a Shinto Shrine*, 81.
23. Nelson, *A Year in the Life of a Shinto Shrine*, 108, 109, 116.
24. De Bary, ed., *Sources of Japanese Tradition Volume I*, 23.
25. Parrinder, *World Religions*, 357.

million followers of Shinto outside of Japan. This makes Shinto the fifth largest religion in the world as of 2020.[26]

Supreme Kami

The most important *kami* (i.e., divine spirit) is *Amaterasu*, the sun goddess who is the divine ancestor of the Imperial Family.[27] She is also considered the Ruler of Heaven.[28] According to Mason, "*Amaterasu* personalizes the all-inclusive oneness of all divine spirit, Heavenly and earthly, according to Shinto."[29] He claimed that not recognizing the superiority of *Amaterasu* is to turn from Shinto principle.[30] According to John Nelson, a professor of East Asian religions in the Department of Theology and Religious Studies at the University of San Francisco, "It is thought that as early as 8th century CE, most of the educated or political elite accepted *Amaterasu* (supreme sun kami) as the central deity...."[31]

Another relevant *kami* to this discussion is *Hachiman*, the Shinto god of warriors, divine protector of Japan and its people, as well as protector of the Imperial Family. *Hachiman* (meaning "eight banners") is one of the most popular Shinto deities in Japan with an estimated half of the registered Shinto shrines dedicated to him. As Helen Hardacre, a professor of Japanese religion and society at Harvard University, explained, main shrines have subordinate branch shrines, which serve to disseminate Shinto to larger numbers of people across wide geographical areas. She noted that in the 1980s, there were twenty-five thousand branch shrines dedicated to *Hachiman*.[32] *Hachiman* is the first *kami* to be credited with using *kamikaze* ("divine wind"), in this case, to disperse invading Mongol fleets of Kublai Khan in the 13th century CE. With the arrival of Buddhism to Japan, *Hachiman* was declared a Buddhist *bodhisattva*, hence, a syncretic deity.

26. https://www.worldatlas.com/articles/largest-religions-in-the-world.html
27. The sun on the Japanese national flag reflects the goddess *Amaterasu*.
28. Mason, *The Meaning of Shinto*, 44.
29. Mason, *The Meaning of Shinto*, 105.
30. Mason, *The Meaning of Shinto*, 105.
31. Nelson, *A Year in the Life of a Shinto Shrine*, 28.
32. Hardacre, *Shinto and the State, 1868-1988*, 11, 13.

Canonical Texts

Shinto has two primary canonical religious texts that do not have the status of sacred texts in the way that the *Vedas* and other Asian religious texts are thought to be inherently holy. They are the *Kojiki* (Records of Ancient Matters) of 712 CE, and the *Nihon-gi* (Chronicles of Japan) of 720 CE. The *Kojiki* is an early Japanese chronicle of myths, legends, songs, genealogies, oral traditions, and semi-historical accounts concerning the origin of the Japanese islands, the *kami*, and the Japanese imperial line. It is the oldest literary work in Japan. As with most sacred religious texts, it contains various songs and poems to make it easier to remember and pass down. The *Nihon-gi* is more elaborate and detailed than the *Kojiki*, and has proven to be an essential reference for Japanese historians. The *Nihon-gi* begins with the Japanese creation myth and covers the first seven generations of divine beings.

Impact of Buddhism

Because of its close proximity to mainland Asia (particularly to China), many cultural influences permeated Japanese society over time, including Confucianism and Buddhism.

However, Confucianism and Buddhism had undergone development for more than one thousand years before they entered Japan.[33] As such, Shinto is also considered a syncretic religion, borrowing from these and other religions.[34]

Buddhism was originally introduced to Korea from China's Fu Jian in 385 CE. From Korea, Buddhism was officially transmitted to Japan when Korean King Seong of the Baekje Kingdom sent a missionary to visit Japanese Emperor Kinmei in 552 CE with gifts, including an image of the Buddha, several Buddhist ritual objects, and Buddhist sacred texts.[35] Prince Shotoku, the first Japanese envoy to China during the Sui Dynasty, described the relationship among the three major religions in Japan as Shinto being the roots of a tree; Confucianism as the trunk of the tree; and Buddhism as the leaves of the tree.[36]

---

33. Mason, *The Meaning of Shinto*, 70.
34. De Bary, ed., *Sources of Japanese Tradition Volume I*, 263.
35. De Bary, ed., *Sources of Japanese Tradition Volume I*, 100.
36. Davies, *Japanese Culture: The Religious and Philosophical Foundations*, 39.

Shinto

Mahayana Buddhism was dominant in China and Korea at that time, so it was the Buddhist tradition that was established in Japan.[37] Because both Shinto and Buddhism were complementary religions (neither religious practice contradicting the other), the Japanese people did not have to pick one religion over the other. As such, most Japanese people today consider themselves as both followers of Shinto *and* Buddhism. Most homes in Japan maintain two home shrines: a *kamidana* for Shinto and a *butsudan* for Buddhism. It is interesting that Shinto considers many Buddhas and *bodhisattvas* to be *kami*, while Buddhism conversely considers many *kami* to be *bodhisattvas* (such as *Hachiman* discussed previously).

Buddhism easily accommodated Shinto and Japanese cultural practices after it was introduced in Japan.[38] Buddhist priests administered both religions in Japan. They participated widely in Shinto rites.[39] Emiko Ohnuki-Teirney, a professor of anthropology at the University of Wisconsin at Madison, provided an example of Shinto and Buddhism working in conjunction with one another. Where Shinto generally focuses on birth and growth, with ceremonies for births and marriages, Buddhism focuses on death and the afterlife, with ceremonies for funerals and memorial services.[40] The union of the two religions was symbolized by the erection of a Buddhist temple next to the Ise Grand Shrine, the most important Shinto shrine in Japan, in 768 CE.[41]

When Buddhism arrived in Japan, the people generally believed it to represent the superior culture of China.[42] As such, in short order, Buddhism became the preferred religion, and Shinto was relegated to minor relative importance—for centuries.[43] Another significant reason for this transformation was that Shinto had so few religious texts to reference that religious education in Japan focused more on Buddhist scripture.[44] Because of its

---

37. Barton, "Buddhism and Shinto: The Two Pillars of Japanese Culture," https://japanology.org/2016/06/buddhism-and-shinto-the-two-pillars-of-japanese-culture/#:~:text=Japan%20is%20home%20to%20not,with%20virtually%20the%20same%20breath; and https://www.japantimes.co.jp/culture/2013/05/16/arts/seeing-where-shinto-and-buddhism-cross/

38. Parrinder, *World's Religions*, 67.

39. Hardacre, *Shinto and the State, 1868-1988*, 13.

40. Davies, *Japanese Culture: The Religious and Philosophical Foundations*, 50.

41. De Bary, ed., *Sources of Japanese Tradition Volume I*, 262.

42. De Bary, ed., *Sources of Japanese Tradition Volume I*, 92.

43. De Bary, ed., *Sources of Japanese Tradition Volume I*, 24.

44. De Bary, ed., *Sources of Japanese Tradition Volume I*, 261.

history and culture, Buddhism inculcated political structure and cultural practices, such as music, dance, art, and a new writing system into Japanese society.[45] As well, Buddhism became a favored religion of the Japanese royal elite because it was perceived as a means of protecting the emperor and imperial family from disease while enhancing their legitimacy with the masses. Despite the royal court preference for Buddhism, local cults of Shinto continued to be the prevailing religion in the rural areas.[46]

As a result of Buddhism being perceived as more superior and established than Shinto, Shinto priests tended to be subordinate to their Buddhist colleagues. One example is that Shinto priests generally sat on the lower seating than Buddhist clerics at village assemblies across the country. As a result, considerable ill-feeling between Shinto and Buddhist priests evolved over the centuries.[47] To counter this inferiority perception relative to Buddhism, senior Shinto priests began to codify Shinto ritual procedures during the 6th and 7th centuries CE.[48]

Let us now discuss how Shinto has been involved in violence and conflict.

---

45. Joseph Kitagawa, "The Buddhist Transformation in Japan," 321

46. Kitagawa, "The Buddhist Transformation in Japan," https://www.journals.uchicago.edu/doi/abs/10.1086/462509

47. Hardacre, *Shinto and the State, 1868-1988*, 13, 15.

48. Nelson, *A Year in the Life of a Shinto Shrine*, 38.

CHAPTER 8

Shinto and Conflict

State Shinto

THE MILITARIZATION OF SHINTO began with the Meiji Restoration in 1868, which ended almost seven hundred years of shogunate rule (i.e., military dictatorship).[1] The army of Prince Tokugawa Yoshinobu, Japan's 15th Shogun, suffered a significant defeat in the Boshin War of 1868, considered a civil war between status quo and progressive factions (who were worried about the technological advances in the West).[2] The victory by the progressive faction led to an empire being created, with Mutsuhito Meiji as its emperor.[3] Helen Hardacre, a professor of Japanese religion and society at Harvard University, defined the term "State Shinto" as the relationship between the Japanese state and the religious practice known as Shinto between 1868 and 1945.[4]

Along with being Japan's 122nd emperor, Meiji was also worshipped as a living god—something common among all Japanese emperors. Emperor Meiji created State Shinto to develop national unity and cultural identity during his modernization of the country.[5] At that time, according the Hardacre, "Shrine Shinto" was perceived as occupying "an ill-defined,

---

1. Hardacre, *Shinto and the State, 1868-1988*, 27.
2. Davies, *Japanese Culture*, 117.
3. Davies, *Japanese Culture*, 115.
4. Hardacre, *Shinto and the State, 1868-1988*, 4.
5. Davies, *Japanese Culture*, 113–114.

residual cultural space lacking positive identification."⁶ In fact, before the Meiji Restoration, Japanese citizens were required to become affiliated with a recognized tradition of Buddhism in order to prevent conversions to Christianity.⁷ After the Meiji Restoration, it became Shinto's function to also unify the hearts and minds of the populace, again, primarily to prevent the spread of Christianity.⁸

As such, State Shinto created the first national calendar, flag, anthem, and standard rituals for all Japanese citizens.⁹ The Japanese government endeavored to formalize Shinto as a religion to be more competitive with Western religions; unify Japanese citizens under State Shinto; and, use State Shinto to support the government in its war efforts.¹⁰ Shinto priesthood also contributed to Japan's expansion of power during this period.¹¹ Shinto ritual placed the emperor in the role of head priest of the nation (analogous to the Catholic pope).¹² The Ise Grand Shrine in Tokyo now became the apex of a pyramidal hierarchy of shrines; their rituals conforming to imperial rites conducted both at the Ise Grand Shrine and in the imperial palace.¹³

State Shinto became the official religion of the Japanese empire that Buddhist leaders were required to accommodate.¹⁴ Shinto became institutionalized by the Meiji government to legitimize his rule and his status as a living deity, analogous to the Buddha. As such, a Department of Shinto was formed (which later expanded into the Ministry of Shinto) that promulgated policies promoting loyalty to the emperor, celebrating Shinto, and restricting the other religions in Japan. The Meiji government used *State* Shinto (in contrast to the traditional *Shrine* Shinto) to promote national patriotism and militarism. As such, all Shinto priests became government

---

6. Hardacre, *Shinto and the State, 1868-1988*, 77.
7. Hardacre, *Shinto and the State, 1868-1988*, 114.
8. Hardacre, *Shinto and the State, 1868-1988*, 89.
9. Hardacre, *Shinto and the State, 1868-1988*, 4.
10. Hardacre, *Shinto and the State, 1868-1988*, 22, 36. Before 1868, shrines operated locally and independently. (Hardacre, *Shinto and the State, 1868-1988*, 100)
11. Hardacre, *Shinto and the State, 1868-1988*, 4.
12. Hardacre, *Shinto and the State, 1868-1988*, 113.
13. Hardacre, *Shinto and the State, 1868-1988*, 104, 28, 32.
14. Davies, *Japanese Culture*, 118; Gier, *The Origins of Religious Violence*, 183.

employees, and all Shinto shrines became government property.[15] State Shinto was also known as *Tennoism* (*Tenno* meaning "heavenly king").[16]

In 1871, Japan's first Ministry of Education was established, and the government began to base its educational policy on Confucian and Shinto values. The minister of education, Mori Arinori, was a central figure in enforcing a nationalistic educational policy and worked out a vast revision of the national school system. Japanese education thereafter tended to be autocratic in nature. All students were required to recite an oath to the imperial family in school every day.[17] As a result, in the following generations, Japan successfully adopted useful aspects of Western education and industry to facilitate rapid modernization.

One of the goals of modernization was to replace the hereditary social hierarchy that was systemic during the shogunate period (1185-1868) with a competitive, merit-based system facilitated by State Shinto and the revised education program.[18] After the Meiji Restoration, the education system was modified to purify Japan from foreign culture and religions in order to facilitate State Shinto. For example, Buddhism was attacked as the religion most to blame for Japan's loss of its original way of life.[19]

The government launched a Great Promulgation Campaign to separate State Shinto from Buddhism as the new state religion. The *Sangha* in Japan complied with the new government direction that Buddhism be relegated to a secondary position relative to new State Shinto. Despite that, government Shinto missionaries still went around Japan to close or destroy four thousand and five hundred Buddhist temples and shrines. Out of the two hundred thousand Buddhist temples in the two hundred and seventy-three years pre-Meiji period, only seventy-four thousand and six hundred survived after the early years of the Meiji period. Buddhist priests and monks were also drafted into the military or forced to become manual laborers.[20] The overall result was that Shinto's identity was increasingly blurred as efforts were made to make it resemble more structured religions. Unfortunately, the Great Teaching and Great Learning programs of the

---

15. Davies, *Japanese Culture*, 118, 120.
16. Parrinder, *World's Religions*, 353.
17. Davies, *Japanese Culture*, 118.
18. Davies, *Japanese Culture*, 113-114.
19. Hardacre, *Shinto and the State, 1868-1988*, 16.
20. Gier, *The Origins of Religious Violence*, 185.

Great Promulgation Campaign did not take hold with the public, resulting in Shinto's image being tarnished.[21]

In 1882, the Meiji government divided Japanese religions into three categories: Buddhism, Christianity, and Shinto. Those citizens who were not Buddhist or Christian were automatically classified as "Shintoists."[22] Additionally, everyone was required to register with their local Shinto shrine, particularly those citizens who had changed residences.[23]

As Japan modernized and its military became stronger, Japan became more aggressive in regional affairs, particularly regarding China, its more powerful neighbor. Japan decided it needed to annex Korea (for strategic and economic reasons) before China did, so Japan invaded the Korean Peninsula, thereby initiating the First Sino-Japanese War with China in 1894. The military conflict was between the Qing Dynasty of China and the Meiji Empire of Japan. China sued for peace in 1895 after six months of military successes by Japanese ground and naval forces. The war demonstrated the success of Japan to modernize, while China was not nearly as successful. Hence, regional dominance in Northeast Asia (NEA) shifted from China to Japan.

In 1904, Russian Tsar Nicholas II decided he needed to seize Port Arthur (a Chinese warm-water port leased by the Russian Navy during the Qing Dynasty), Manchuria, and Korea. As a result of this Russian aggression, Japan declared war and fought with Russian forces in northeastern China and on the seas around the Korean Peninsula. During this war, Shinto priests were expected to serve the nation in fostering patriotism. As a result of government support, Shinto priests became more numerous and better trained.[24] When Japan defeated Russia in what is now called the Russo-Japanese War of 1904–5, State Shinto was given much of the credit, hence, became an even more significant influence within Japan.[25]

Following this major military victory over Russia, numerous Shinto sects began forming throughout Japan. The Meiji government recognized more than thirteen Shinto sects.[26] However, Japanese officials became

21. Hardacre, *Shinto and the State, 1868-1988*, 42-50.
22. Parrinder, *World Religions*, 375.
23. Hardacre, *Shinto and the State, 1868-1988*, 29.
24. Hardacre, *Shinto and the State, 1868-1988*, 23.
25. Gier, *The Origins of Religious Violence*, 186.
26. Garon, "State and Religion in Imperial Japan, 1912-1945," 273.

Shinto and Conflict

worried that many of these sects were actually pseudo-religions and evil cults led by communists. As such, many of the new Shinto sect leaders were eventually arrested.[27] Then, the Second Sino-Japanese War began in 1937 when a minor dispute between Japanese and Chinese troops in China escalated into a full-scale invasion by Japan. (This war eventually became attached to World War II.)

In 1937, the Meiji government began shutting down numerous Shinto, Buddhist, and Christian sects because of the Second Sino-Japanese War. At the same time, the government began conscripting members of the various religions to support the war effort and passing laws to regulate all religions even more closely. For example, the Buddhist *Orders* in Japan were required to cut their number in half.[28] According to Hardacre, Japan also implemented a policy of one Shinto shrine per village, resulting in over eighty-one thousand civic shrines being eliminated. These mergers drastically changed the character of local shrine life and confused the people. Again, State Shinto lost even more respect due to the government's radical policies.[29]

In 1939, all religions in Japan were placed directly under the emperor, and in 1940, State Shinto became law within the empire, officially making Japan a theocracy.[30] The bottom line is that State Shinto was created to suppress the political power of Shrine Shinto and Buddhism in Japan while increasing the power of the Meiji regime. State Shinto was exploited by the Imperial Government to support Japan's expansionist policies in the Pacific Ocean and the war effort against the United States.[31]

In February 1944, with the tide of the war in the Pacific turning against Japan, Emperor Hirohito authorized suicide missions by both the Army and Navy. By late 1944, Japan had weaponized Shinto to inspire and motivate *kamikaze* aerial squadrons. The volunteer *kamikaze* pilots believed they were involved in a holy war and that their divine emperor had sanctioned the policy to use them as "special" suicide weapons. This did not cause much resistance as suicide was viewed as a great honor by

---

27. Garon, "State and Religion in Imperial Japan, 1912-1945," 273.
28. Garon, "State and Religion in Imperial Japan, 1912-1945," 279, 300.
29. Hardacre, *Shinto and the State, 1868-1988*, 39, 98, 99.
30. Garon, "State and Religion in Imperial Japan, 1912-1945," 301; Hardacre, *Shinto and the State*, 40.
31. Hardacre, *Shinto and the State, 1868-1988*, 40.

Buddhist Samurai.³² Another form of ritual suicide was called *hara-kiri*. It was associated with Shinto by way of the Samurai code of honor. *Hara-kiri* is intended to cleanse one of shame incurred through bad judgment or ill will and reinstate honor to the family name.³³

With the military defeat of Japan, State Shinto was outlawed by the 1945 Shinto Directive. Consequently, Shrine Shinto slowly began to make a comeback. However, Shinto, in general, was discredited by Japan's loss in World War II, and its priests were genuinely concerned that General MacArthur would impose Christianity upon Japan to preclude future militarism.³⁴ One indication of this was after World War II, all Shinto shrines, including Yasukuni,³⁵ lost government funding and were placed on the same legal basis as all other religious organizations.³⁶

At the end of World War II (to include the Second Sino-Japanese War), State Shinto could be associated with the deaths of up to twenty million people in China, up to one million people in the Philippines, and over four hundred thousand people in Korea (to cite a few of the affected countries).³⁷ This figure is far higher than the total deaths associated with Christianity (to include the Crusades and Inquisition). By themselves, religions such as Shinto, Buddhism, and Christianity are relatively peaceful. It is only when they were married to government and political policymaking that they turned exceptionally deadly.

Moving to the 21st century, the population of Japan has become much more urban over the decades, much to the detriment of Shinto and its shrines. As well, the demographic of Japan indicates an aging society, meaning the elderly are primarily the ones left to care for the Shinto shrines. In fact, most Shinto shrines are largely ignored by parishioners except for annual festivals, weddings, and tourists.³⁸

---

32. Jerryson and Juergensmeyer, eds., *Buddhist Warfare*, 14 fn, 47.
33. Frank, *Downfall*, 319–20.
34. Hardacre, *Shinto and the State, 1868-1988*, 142, 135.
35. The Yasukuni Shrine in Tokyo is a national shrine for its war dead much like Arlington Cemetery is for the United States.
36. Hardacre, *Shinto and the State, 1868-1988*, 133.
37. https://www.nationalww2museum.org/students-teachers/student-resources/research-starters/research-starters-worldwide-deaths-world-war
38. Hardacre, *Shinto and the State, 1868-1988*, 142, 163.

Shinto and Conflict

Interestingly, Hardacre determined that the legacy of State Shinto *has persisted* until the present. Since 1945, Shinto and the state have succeeded in reconstituting parts of the symbolic edifice that once united them.[39] The seeds have been planted in Japan for history to repeat itself yet again in the future.

At this point, we have discussed each of the three major religions in Asia and how each accommodated violence and conflict. Now, we will compare and contrast the Asian religions with the Abrahamic religions for similarities and differences. After that, we will examine how the religions of the East and West facilitated violence and conflict in similar and different approaches.

---

39. Hardacre, *Shinto and the State, 1868-1988*, 4, 163.

CHAPTER 9

Comparing Religions

THIS SECTION WILL FIRST analyze the three selected Asian religions among themselves, then analyze the Asian religions with two of the three Abrahamic religions (leaving out Judaism as it does not apply). The purpose of these analyses is to better understand each of the Asian religions relative to the Abrahamic religions, as well as set the stage for a similar analysis regarding how each of them facilitates conflict (in the next chapter).

Asian Religions

The main reason that Hinduism, Buddhism, Jainism, and Sikhism have so much in common is that they are all syncretic religions sourcing back to the ancient Indian Vedas.[1] (Note that Shinto does not source back to the Vedas, but rather to ancient Japanese traditions and culture.)

Hinduism and Buddhism

Hinduism and Buddhism have a lot in common as religions, much as Catholicism and Protestantism have a lot in common. According to Kaushik Roy, a professor at the Jadavpur University in Calcutta, India, Buddhism drew its lifeblood from Hinduism and morphed into an "Indian Protestantism."[2] This makes sense given that Gautama, the Shakyamuni Buddha, was originally a Hindu (analogous to Jesus being a Jew). Gautama

---

1. Varshney, *Ethnic Conflict and Civic Life Hindus and Muslims in India*, 65.
2. Roy, *Hinduism and the Ethics of Warfare in South Asia*, 92.

appears to have adopted many aspects of the *Upanishads* during his search for the solution to human suffering. For example, the fundamental principles of Buddhism, including the *dharma,* karma, reincarnation based on merit, and *Nirvana* (release from the cycle of rebirth), are similar in Hinduism.[3] Another example is that the Hindu god/avatar Rama found his way into Buddhist literature.[4] Where the Buddhist *Jataka* text (part of the Pali canon) portrays Rama as an incarnation of the Buddha in a previous life, Hindu texts portray the Buddha as an avatar of the Hindu god *Vishnu*.[5] These two religions also peacefully co-existed in India for many centuries. According to Nicholas Gier, a professor of philosophy at the University of Idaho, Hindu-Buddhist harmony began as early as 200 BCE. He further noted that even Burmese kings who were Buddhists integrated Hindu rituals into their worship and even honored Muslims.[6]

It is also useful to analyze where the two syncretic religions differ. The Hindu religion is aimed toward uniting the overarching essence of the universe to one's individual soul (*atman*), whereas Buddhism is about finding the "not soul" (*anatman*). In Hinduism, attaining the highest life is a process of removing the bodily distractions from life, allowing one to eventually understand the nature of Brahman. In Buddhism, one follows a disciplined life to understand that there is nothing in oneself (i.e., not "me" or "I") such that one dispels the illusion of existence. In so doing, one realizes *Nirvana*.[7]

Despite the clear syncretic nature of Hinduism and Buddhism, Gautama denied all authority of the Brahmin scriptures, indicating they were useless.[8] Finally, unlike Hindus, Buddhists do not find any merit in devotion to a pantheon of deities, doing formal rituals performed by priests, or most significantly, accepting the caste system. According to Heinz Bechert, a former professor of Buddhism at the Georg-August University in Gottingen, there have been mass conversions to Buddhism throughout India because of the Hindu-sanctioned caste system.[9]

---

3. Roy, *Hinduism and the Ethics of Warfare in South Asia,* xiii; Doniger, *On Hinduism,* 4.
4. Cook, *Ancient Religions, Modern Politics,* 66.
5. Holt, The Buddhist Viṣṇu: Religious Transformation, Politics, and Culture, 18–21.
6. Gier, *The Origins of Religious Violence,* 113.
7. https://www.diffen.com/difference/Buddhism_vs_Hinduism
8. Bechert and Gombrich, eds., *The World of Buddhism,* 12.
9. Bechert and Gombrich, eds., *The World of Buddhism,* 278.

Buddhism and Shinto

In Japan, Shinto did not adopt many Buddhist principles and practices as much as it simply co-existed with Buddhism. Most Japanese people consider themselves as both followers of Shinto as well as *Mahayana* Buddhists. Their holy places (i.e., Shinto shrines and Buddhist temples) are primarily to pray and meditate at any time. However, there is one significant difference between these two religions. Buddhists believe in a cycle of death and rebirth that continues until a person achieves the enlightened state of *Nirvana*. Shinto tradition holds that after death, the deceased *kami* passes on to another world to watch over any descendants. This is one reason why ancestor veneration is still an important part of modern-day Japanese culture.

Shinto and Hinduism

One of the few commonalities between Shinto and Hinduism is that followers of Shinto adopted some of the more prominent Hindu gods to worship, including *Shiva*, *Brahman*, and *Indra*. The only other commonality is that neither religion has an acknowledged founder, such as the Apostle Paul for Christianity or the Prophet Muhammad for Islam. The tradition and culture do not require a human founder as the foundations of the tradition are placed in a mythological narrative. The Venn diagram below summarizes the commonalities between these three religions.

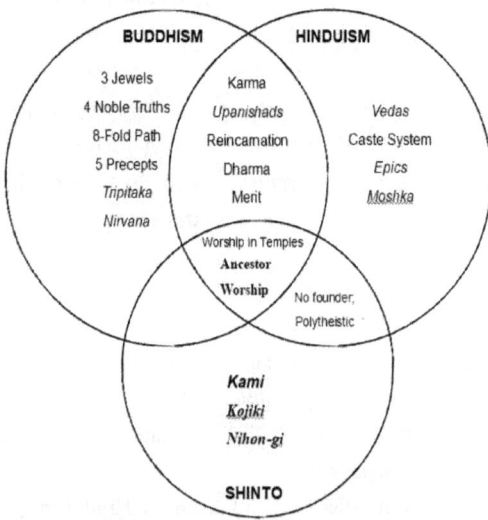

Venn Diagram of Selected Asian Religions[10]

10. Author created.

Asian vs. Abrahamic Religions

To begin, let me offer some general observations about the Far Eastern versus Western religions. The Abrahamic religions of Judaism, Christianity, and Islam have a great deal more institutional infrastructure and a clear organizational hierarchy in comparison to most other religions around the world. Each has one supreme deity; one human founder or prophet; and one primary sacred text that has been canonized. Each of the Abrahamic religions has established a hierarchy of authority; religious observances to be performed on a weekly basis; and recognized processes and accompanying rites of passage to signify conversion to their religions.[11] The Asian religions being analyzed here (and representing other ones with fewer adherents) generally do not have these things. For example, Jewish, Christian, and Muslim congregations stress the value of regular communal worship and social service, where there is no obligation for a Hindu or Buddhist even to visit a temple.[12] However, according to Geoffrey Parrinder, a Methodist minister and professor at King's College in London, while Asian religions have little organization compared to the Abrahamic religions, they do have a few things in common, such as Hinduism having priests, and Buddhism having a Buddha and the *Sangha*.[13]

As such, the Asian religions tend not to have as much perceived legitimacy as the Abrahamic religions, even though they have a much longer history.[14] Michael Cook, a professor of Near Eastern Studies at Princeton University, concluded that both Hindu ethnic and religious identities were considerably weaker than those within Islam.[15] On the other hand, he also noted that "Hindu heritage is considerably more comprehensive than that of Islam."[16] As for the primary philosophical difference between Eastern and Western religions, Nicholas Gier, a professor of philosophy at the University of Idaho, found that the Abrahamic religions focused on "Ought"

---

11. Juergensmeyer, Kitts, and Jerryson, eds., *Violence and the World's Religious Traditions*, 39.

12. Parrinder, *World Religions*, 19.

13. Bechert and Gombrich, *The World of Buddhism*, 138; Cook, *Ancient Religions, Modern Politics*, 19.

14. Buddhism/Hinduism/Shinto are ancient religions, older than Christianity and Islam. (Lehr, *Militant Buddhism*, 32–33)

15. Cook, *Ancient Religions, Modern Politics*, 70.

16. Cook, *Ancient Religions, Modern Politics*, 294.

(threat of punishment) while the Asian religions focused on "Is" (focus on reward).[17]

When in competition with one another in Asia, the indigenous religions tended to lose followers to the newer Abrahamic religions (primarily to Islam and then to Christianity). Often, the newer religions were part of foreign civilizations that were perceived as more advanced at the time. Heinz Bechert and Cho Sungtaek, a professor of philosophy at Korea University in Seoul, both noted, for example, that by the early 16th century, Buddhism was threatened by Christian missionaries.[18]

Often a country that was conquered in war had a new religion forced upon the population. In other cases, due to trade, foreign nations appeared to be more advanced and cultured. Adopting the new religion was often perceived as a way to ingratiate oneself with foreigners or occupiers, who were generally in positions of authority. According to Bechert, converting to Christianity brought Indians many privileges from the British colonialists.[19] Doniger noted that Hindus so admired their British rulers that it reflected a kind of colonial or religious Stockholm syndrome.[20] For the most part, most religions co-existed peacefully with one another in Asia for centuries. Gier noted that in Asia, citizens celebrated the syncretism of their religions, which allowed for the widespread tolerance of other religions. His cited example was Korean Reverend Moon, who was celebrated as being a Protestant, a Buddhist, and a Korean Shaman.[21] He also pointed out that unlike the Abrahamic religions, Hindu kings formed political and religious alliances with *tribal* chiefs and priests often resulting in further religious syncretism.[22]

This section will compare and contrast each of the Asian religions in four distinct topic areas: 1) champions, 2) sacred texts, 3) proselytizing, and 4) fundamentalism. Of the six religions to be analyzed, Christianity and Hinduism/Buddhism have the most in common. Gier concluded that

17. Gier, *The Origins of Religious Violence*, 241.
18. Bechert and Gombrich, eds., *The World of Buddhism*, 273; Tikhonov and Brekke, eds., *Buddhism and Violence*, 56.
19. Bechert and Gombrich, eds., *The World of Buddhism*, 273.
20. Doniger, *On Hinduism*, 16. Stockholm syndrome is a psychological response by the conquered victims that occurs over a period of time where victims bond with their captors. With this syndrome, victims may come to sympathize with their captors and even come to develop positive feelings towards them.
21. Gier, *The Origins of Religious Violence*, 246.
22. Gier, *The Origins of Religious Violence*, 4.

Buddhist philosophy was more in line with the Abrahamic religions,[23] while Myrtle Langley, an author of world religions, determined that *Mahayana* Buddhism "coincided" with Christianity.[24] The ultimate goal of these religions is very similar. For Christians, the goal is freedom from the bondage of sin and material decay, while for Hindus, it is to be freed from the suffering of death and rebirth.

It is important to note that there are commonalities between Islam and Buddhism, and between Islam and Hinduism, too.[25] This makes sense when one considers that Islam is an outgrowth from Christianity, and Buddhism is an evolution of Hinduism. Peter Lehr, a research fellow at the University of Saint Andrews, determined that *Theravada* Buddhism is most comparable to the *Sunni* sect of Islam.[26] As well, both Islam and Buddhism peacefully co-existed in northern India for centuries.[27]

Champions

Christianity and Buddhism both have an identified champion who was deified after death. Both Gautama and Jesus were pressured during their lives to be considered as deities, which they both resisted. Once they died, such efforts were more successful.[28]

Swami Dayananda Saraswati (1824-1883) is best known for founding the *Arya Samaj* ("Society of Nobles"), a Hindu reform movement in 1875. This group advocated the belief in God as the supreme form of religion. As such, *Arya Samaj* decreed that Hinduism had always been monotheistic, with Brahman being its creator god. As well, *Arya Samaj* decreed the *Upanishads* (its counterpart to the Bible) advocated for one god.[29] Swami Dayananda declared that any contrary views were due to post-Vedic "degenerative developments and to textual misinterpretation."[30]

23. Gier, *The Origins of Religious Violence*, 241.
24. Langley, *World Religions*, 30.
25. Doniger determined that Catholicism resembled Hinduism in many ways (Doniger, *On Hinduism*, 15).
26. Lehr, *Militant Buddhism*, 108.
27. Smith, *The World's Religions*, 107.
28. Smith, *The World's Religions*, 90.
29. Doniger, *On Hinduism*, 15.
30. Gier, *The Origins of Religious Violence*, 275.

Both Gautama and Jesus began preaching earnestly at the age of twenty-nine.[31] The future Buddhas and Jesus's future return would purify the world.[32] Regarding the future return of the Buddha, the Sixth Buddhist Council held in Rangoon, Burma, predicted his arrival in 1956, the 2500th anniversary of Shakyamuni Buddha's *Nirvana*.[33] On the other hand, Jesus performed miracles before Gentiles in hopes they would believe in his teachings and follow him, while Gautama did not believe in miracles.[34] According to Etienne Lamotte, a Belgian priest and professor who taught at Catholic University in Louvain, "Buddha did not do miracles to demonstrate the validity of his teachings."[35] The greatest irony is that while Gautama the Buddha and Jesus preached peace and non-violence, their followers committed some of the most religiously-motivated violence in world history.[36]

Sacred Texts

The Asian sacred text that comes closest to the Bible as far as being canonized, content, and purpose, is the Hindu *Upanishads*. According to Gier, Dayananda argued that the *Upanishads* (with its Vedic texts) is equivalent to the Bible.[37] In *Theravada* Buddhism, the most sacred text is the *Tripitaka*, the triple baskets of Pali Canon consisting of Discipline, Sayings, and Philosophy baskets. Gombrich observed that Buddhist Canon "consisted of Three Baskets of texts equivalent of the Bible for Christians or the [*Qur'an*] for Muslims."[38] While the British ruled over India, the Hindus tried to recast Hinduism to be more legitimate in the eyes of their conquerors, citing the *Bhagavad Gita* as its Bible.[39]

A significant issue with the Bible has been the numerous edits, redactions, translations, and modifications applied to it over the centuries after it

---

31. Bechert and Gombrich, eds., *The World of Buddhism*, 41.

32. De Bary ed., *Sources of Chinese Tradition Volume 1*, 270.

33. Bechert and Gombrich, eds., *The World of Buddhism*, 156. No new Buddha appeared in 1956.

34. Bechert and Gombrich, eds., *The World of Buddhism*, 45.

35. Bechert and Gombrich, eds., *The World of Buddhism*, 45.

36. Gier, *The Origins of Religious Violence*, 275.

37. Gier, *The Origins of Religious Violence*, 244.

38. Bechert and Gombrich, eds., *The World of Buddhism*, 77.

39. Doniger, *On Hinduism*, 16.

was canonized at the Council of Nicaea in 325 CE. Something similar occurred to the Buddhist holy texts. A reinterpretation of the Buddha's words often occurred after the Buddhist canon was written down *centuries after the Buddha's death.* (Prior to that, it was an oral tradition that required monks to memorize the sacred texts.[40] Of course, monks' memories were fallible; meaning accuracy was also fallible.) Gil Fronsdal, a Zen Buddhist who teaches at the Insight Meditation Center in Redwood City, California, concluded that "ancient Buddhist editors made many verse anthologies. The process of selecting, excluding, and arranging the verses continued over an extended period of time within diverse Buddhist communities."[41] Examining the *Dhammapada*, he found that "Although many of the verses originated with the Buddha, the evidence argues *against* the claim that they have all so originated."[42] As well, Fronsdal discovered that among various *Dhammapada* texts, "the chapters and verses appear in very different orders."[43] Bechert found that the Fifth and Sixth Buddhist Councils made textual revisions of the Buddhist scriptures, much like various Christian Ecumenical Councils did to the Bible for hundreds of years.[44]

While the Abrahamic religions now focus on a literal interpretation of the sacred texts, the Asian religions are much more ambiguous regarding their various sacred scriptures. According to Lehr, "In literal tradition, faithfulness to the Buddha's teaching no longer necessitates *a strictly literal adherence* to his actual words but may also be based upon views which follow the spirit of the Buddha's teaching."[45] Lehr determined that Buddhist scripture also tended to be a bit ambiguous as a result of inaccurate transcriptions and translations.[46]

Whenever something is translated, there are inaccuracies in the translation as languages are all different from one another – some more than others. Initially, when Buddhist scripture needed to be translated into Chinese, there were no translators qualified to do this.[47] Once Chinese translations were finally done, Theodore de Bary, formerly an East Asian scholar

---

40. Lehr, *Militant Buddhism*, 62.
41. Fronsdal, *The Dhammapada*, 110.
42. Fronsdal, *The Dhammapada*, 112.
43. Fronsdal, *The Dhammapada*, 113.
44. Bechert and Gombrich, eds., *The World of Buddhism*, 154.
45. Lehr, *Militant Buddhism*, 63.
46. Lehr, *Militant Buddhism*, 82.
47. Lehr, *Militant Buddhism*, 197.

and professor at Columbia University, noted that "Buddhist text translated into Chinese was the word of Buddha—even if there were *frequent glaring inconsistencies*."[48] (In any case, it was difficult for Chinese people to assimilate Buddhism due to textual, linguistic, conceptual, and historical reasons.[49]) Fronsdal explained that "A translator often has to strike a balance between literal but clumsy language and elegant but inaccurate language."[50]

In Asia, the tradition regarding holy texts was not to include the names of authors or dates of publication. In ancient Chinese history, there is uncertainty regarding publication dates, authors, numbers, and even facts. For example, numbers were often used not as data but to convey impressions, much like in the Arab culture (e.g., 40 meant "a lot" or "too many to count").[51]

Proselytizing

Hinduism and Shinto are indigenous religions that are also part of the ethnic and cultural composition of India and Japan, respectively. As such, these religions did not expand much beyond their origin countries over the millennia. They did not proselytize as other global religions did. According to Roy, it was primarily due to geographical factors that India did not have any extraterritorial ambitions (though this was not the same for Japan).[52] However, where Hinduism was never threatened with extinction, Shinto almost succumbed to the invasions of both Christianity and Buddhism in Japan. It successfully reacted to this perceived threat by improving its native identity.[53]

Regarding Buddhism, it slowly expanded eastward into China and Japan along the established trade routes as well as southward to most of Southeast Asia. However, it did not expand by military force as Islam did, nor was it looking to become a global religion as Christianity and Islam have become.[54] While the Buddha exhorted his followers to spread the

---

48. De Bary, ed., *Sources of Chinese Tradition Volume 1*, 287.
49. De Bary, ed., *Sources of Chinese Tradition Volume 1*, 290.
50. Fronsdal, *The Dhammapada*, xii.
51. Fronsdal, *The Dhammapada*, 7, 8.
52. Roy, *Hinduism and the Ethics of Warfare in South Asia*, 243.
53. Tikhonov and Brekke, eds., *Buddhism and Violence*, 56.
54. Gier, *The Origins of Religious Violence*, 249; Tikhonov and Brekke, eds., *Buddhism and Violence*, 177.

dharma peacefully,[55] Nichiren Buddhism called for *shakubuku* – "forceful proselytism."[56] For the Buddha, expanding the faith was critical for Buddhism to endure. As such, proselytizing was an essential duty for monks to regenerate the *Sangha* and recruit new monks for Buddhist monasteries.[57] The main threats to the expansion of Buddhism were the two global Abrahamic religions – Christianity and Islam. Islam arrived in India around the middle of the seventh century CE.[58] Buddhism eventually disappeared from India by 1300 CE due to the military successes of Islamic forces that had entered India from Afghanistan.[59] The destruction of the great Buddhist university at Nalanda, India, by Muslim invaders around 1200 CE signified the beginning of the end for Buddhism in India.

Christianity, India's third most followed religion, arrived in India in the 2nd century CE. Two ancient testimonies exist about the mission of Saint Bartholomew to India; Eusebius of Caesarea (early 4th century) and Saint Jerome (late 4th century). Eusebius of Caesarea's Ecclesiastical History (5:10) states that after the ascension of Jesus to heaven, Apostle Bartholomew went on a missionary tour to India, where he preached the Gospels and left behind a copy of the Gospel of Matthew.[60] Protestantism was later spread throughout India by the efforts of North American, British, German, and independent missionaries. Lehr pointed out that in response to the Christian missionary proselytizing efforts in Asia, many younger monks adopted *Theravada* Buddhism as a counter to Christianity.[61]

While China still has more Buddhists than any other country in the world, and while Buddhism is the largest religion in China today, Buddhism had a more challenging time being accepted than Chinese indigenous religions, such as Daoism and Confucianism. As Buddhism entered China (likely during the 1st century CE from India), it encountered a massive empire (the Han Dynasty) with over a thousand years of civilization. Gombrich noted that "it was hard for Buddhism with its doctrine of individual salvation to affect it."[62]

55. Lehr, *Militant Buddhism*, 36.
56. Parrinder, *World Religions*, 369.
57. Lehr, *Militant Buddhism*, 84.
58. Doniger, *On Hinduism*, 13.
59. Bechert and Gombrich, eds., *The World of Buddhism*, 273.
60. https://www.nasrani.net/2007/02/13/saint-bartholomew-mission-in-india/
61. Lehr, *Militant Buddhism*, 107.
62. Bechert and Gombrich, eds., *The World of Buddhism*, 193.

Today, China is a communist country. Karl Marx, the father of communism, wrote in 1843 that religion is the opiate of the masses, giving them false hope.[63] However, Article 36 of the Chinese Constitution says that citizens "enjoy freedom of religious belief."[64] The State Council passed regulations on religious affairs in 2017 to allow religious organizations to possess property, publish literature, train and approve clergy, and collect donations. However, these measures do not guarantee the right to practice or worship. As well, alongside these rights come heightened government controls. Finally, while religious belief in China is protected by its Constitution, China ostensibly recognizes just five religions: Buddhism, Daoism, Catholicism, Protestantism, and Islam.[65] (Note: Of the five religions, only Daoism is native to China.)

Fundamentalism

Fundamentalist movements within most religions around the world have been motivated by the perceived threat of the advances of modernization and by the growing separation of church and state (i.e., secularization). Secularization causes religion to lose the authority to develop and implement political policy or to require people to follow religious policies.[66] According to Gabriel Almond, a professor of political science for multiple universities, to include Yale, Princeton, and Stanford, "These [fundamentalist] movements are militant and highly focused antagonists of secularization. They follow the rule of offense being better than defense."[67]

Fundamentalist leaders decide which scriptures to reference to support their cause, making their efforts illegitimate and often extremist.[68] Selengut determined that charismatic religious leaders are also unpredictable.

---

63. The quotation originates from the introduction of Karl Marx's work A Contribution to the Critique of Hegel's Philosophy of Right, https://www.marxists.org/archive/marx/works/1843/critique-hpr/intro.htm

64. http://www.china.org.cn/e-white/Freedom/f-2.htm#:~:text=Article%2036%20of%20the%20Constitution,they%20discriminate%20against%20citizens%20who

65. https://www.state.gov/reports/2019-report-on-international-religious-freedom/china/#:~:text=The%20government%20recognizes%20five%20official,Islam%2C%20Protestantism%2C%20and%20Catholicism.

66. Selengut, *Sacred Fury*, 157.

67. Almond, Appleby, and Sivan, *Strong Religion*, 2.

68. Almond, Appleby, and Sivan, *Strong Religion*, 17, 18.

They do not follow conventional religious rules or ask for approval from religious peers or official religious bodies.[69]

Where fundamentalism arose within Protestantism in the late 19th century, it also arose in both Hinduism (see *Hindutva*) and in Buddhism (see *Theravada* tradition). According to Doniger, "as fundamentalism raised its ugly head among the major monotheisms (Judaism, Christianity, and Islam), Hinduism in India caught it, too. The movement known as *Hindutva* ('Hindu-ness'), while protesting that it is a reaction against European pressures, it actually mimics Protestant evangelical strategies, including fundamentalist agendas."[70]

European imperialism and colonialism inspired the rise of religious nationalism and fundamentalism in Asia.[71] The British Empire in India sparked the emergence of fundamentalism within Hinduism and other Asian religions.[72] The Hindu fundamentalist movement coincided with the nationalist movement within India, beginning with the *Arya Samaj* group. It sought to replace India's secular constitution with something based on *Hindutva*.[73] As well, Hindu nationalists had no problem asking all Hindus to turn toward Ayodhya, the birthplace of Lord Rama,[74] when praying (much as Muslims turn toward Mecca when praying).[75] According to Almond, "The *Hindutva* movement in India borrows elements from theistic traditions of the West including a supernatural founder (Lord Rama) with a contested birthplace (Ayodhya) in order to give Hinduism credibility."[76]

Within Buddhism, fundamentalism meant eliminating syncretic accretions, such as various gods, magic, and sorcery, and returning to just

---

69. Selengut, *Sacred Fury*, 230.

70. Doniger, *On Hinduism*, 19.

71. Gier, *The Origins of Religious Violence*, 252.

72. Almond, Appleby, and Sivan, *Strong Religion*, 174.

73. Almond, Appleby, and Sivan, *Strong Religion*, 176.

74. Brahma or Rama is the name given to the highest god; the other highest gods are Vishnu and Shiva.
https://quod.lib.umich.edu/d/did/did2222.0003.316/--rama-or-brahma?rgn=main;view=fulltext;q1=Paul+Henri+Dietrich%2C+baron+d++Holbach+ascribed; Cook, *Ancient Religions, Modern Politics*, 295.

75. Cook, *Ancient Religions, Modern Politics*, 426.

76. Almond, Appleby, and Sivan, *Strong Religion*, 16.

Theravada Buddhism.[77] (Note that *Theravada* is orthodox Buddhism that stresses the withdrawal from worldly values, including politics.[78])

Other Commonalities

Naturally, there are many other commonalities among these religions that could fill volumes. Of note, pilgrimages are not exclusive to Islam (with its *Hajj* requirement for all Muslims to visit Mecca at least once in their lives). Hinduism and Buddhism have a set of large-scale pilgrimages that take place periodically. For example, every twelve years, Hindus travel to sites mentioned in the epic *Mahabharata* or the *Puranas*. In 1968, the Hindu pilgrimage was to Badrinath.[79] As for daily worship, Hindu worship to Brahman includes three daily offerings compared to the five times a day prayer to Allah for all Muslims.[80] With the religion comparisons completed, let us now assess how the Asian religions accommodate conflict compared to the Abrahamic religions (specifically, Christianity and Islam).

---

77. Almond, Appleby, and Sivan, *Strong Religion*, 165.
78. Almond, Appleby, and Sivan, *Strong Religion*, 165.
79. Cook, *Ancient Religions, Modern Politics*, 69.
80. Parrinder, *World Religions*, 194.

CHAPTER 10

Comparing Religion and Conflict

THIS CHAPTER WILL COMPARE Christianity and Islam with the three Asian religions regarding religious violence and conflict. Given that civilizations, societies, and countries are different as a function of geography, time, weather, history, culture, language, and religious beliefs, then it is logical to believe that religious violence and conflict around the world should have little in common with one another. As such, it may be more interesting to analyze *the similarities* among polities regarding religious violence and conflict. To accomplish this analysis, I will compare each of the Asian religions discussed with each one of the Abrahamic religions (not including Judaism) regarding violence and conflict, including Hinduism vs. Islam, Hinduism vs. Christianity, Buddhism vs. Islam, Buddhism vs. Christianity, and Shinto vs. Christianity. As a bonus, I will include one final comparison of religious fundamentalism and conflict: Islamic vs. Hindu fundamentalism.

Hinduism vs. Islam

Beginning with Hinduism, its sacred texts are filled with violence and conflict, more so than Buddhism. Charles Selengut, professor of sociology at Drew University, determined that both Hinduism and Buddhism had incorporated elements of holy war in their religions.[1] However, Cook found that Hinduism's canonical texts were full of martial violence as compared to Buddhism.[2] This reflection of conflict and violence in Hinduism is

1. Selengut, *Sacred Fury*, 21.
2. Cook, *Ancient Religions, Modern Politics*, 235.

analogous to the content of Islam's sacred texts. As such, the scriptures of Hinduism and Islam readily accommodate violence, reflecting their respective civilization's long histories of conflict (part of the Hindu and Arab cultures, respectively). For example, Kaushik Roy, a professor at Jadavpur University in Calcutta, India, found that Islamic epic literature of this time emphasized Muslim victories, while Hindu counter-epics emphasized resistance and repudiation of Islam.[3] The primary difference between Hinduism and Islam regarding conflict is that Hinduism does not seek to proselytize beyond South Asia, whereas Islam promotes the concept of *Dar al-Harb* – those lands not under Islamic rule that still need to be conquered and assimilated. In fact, as a result of the numerous Muslim terrorist attacks around the world since 1980, the common perception is that Muslims are pursuing Islamic world domination.[4] As well, there is a distinct advantage when a religion is global (like Islam) over one that is primarily regional (like Hinduism) if only because of the greater opportunity for global religions to project power and mobilize resources across national borders.[5]

When Islam spread to Central and South Asia, Hinduism was not able to prevent it. Nicholas Gier, a professor of philosophy at the University of Idaho, found that "A weakened Hinduism was easy prey for Muslim invaders and then British imperialism."[6] Before the incursion of Islam, India did not have an established monolithic religion. As well, at that time, Hinduism consisted of many various sects and cults that often fought with one another, desecrating each other's temples along the way.[7] As mentioned earlier, many religious scholars believed that Hinduism's assimilation of significant parts of pacifist Buddhism weakened it, making Hinduism more susceptible to defeat.

For the first time, India was confronted with a religious invader it could not assimilate, whose rulers had access to an established religious and cultural tradition of their own.[8] So, instead of Hinduism assimilating Islam as it had all other religions in South Asia, Islam *replaced* Hinduism in India beginning in 1206 CE for over six centuries. Moreover, while many

---

3. Roy, *Hinduism and the Ethics of Warfare in South Asia*, 162.
4. Gunasingham, "Buddhist Extremism in Sri Lanka and Myanmar," 1.
5. Lehr, *Militant Buddhism*, 24.
6. Gier, *The Origins of Religious Violence*, 28.
7. Roy, *Hinduism and the Ethics of Warfare in South Asia*, 174.
8. Cook, *Ancient Religions, Modern Politics*, 231.

Hindus were forced to convert to Islam once their region was conquered, most Muslims living in India were never forced to convert to Hinduism.[9]

In the late 19th century, Hinduism began making a comeback against Islam with *Hindutva*. *Hindutva* recognized the *Upanishads* as Hinduism's most sacred text and Brahman as its supreme deity, thereby giving it more legitimacy when compared to the Abrahamic religions. (However, due to India's excessive population, individuality was downplayed in favor of family, tribes, groups, and castes. Consequently, there is no individual prophet figure regarding Hinduism.) As such, *Hindutva* adherents began to attack Muslims in the northern and western regions of India beginning in the 20th century.[10] Muslims often retaliated by attacking cows—animals considered sacred in Hinduism.[11] Cow protection campaigns were launched in 1893, 1952, and 1967, which further ignited Hindu-Muslim hostilities.[12]

The Hindu riots and pogroms against Muslims in India have become common.[13] India's Hindu-Muslim violence is city-oriented and locally concentrated.[14] Despite significant attempts by the BJP leadership to spread the violence throughout India, the religious violence has barely touched the rural areas, remaining in large part in the major cities in India. According to Ashutosh Varshney, a professor of political science and international relations at Brown University, more than half of all religion-related deaths have been in just eight of India's four hundred cities.[15]

Some scholars believe that if Hindus and Muslims cooperated more at a local level in communal settings, then such riots would be less likely to occur.[16] Varshney found that "Where social networks of engagement existed at the local level, tensions and conflict were regulated and managed; where they are missing, communal identities led to endemic violence."[17]

On the other hand, Paul Brass, a professor of political science at the University of Washington, discovered that riots also served a political

---

9. Gier, *The Origins of Religious Violence*, 9.
10. Varshney, *Ethnic Conflict and Civic Life Hindus and Muslims in India*, 6.
11. Cook, *Ancient Religions, Modern Politics*, 63–64.
12. Cook, *Ancient Religions, Modern Politics*, 296.
13. Brass, *The Production of Hindu-Muslim Violence in Contemporary India*, 6.
14. Varshney *Ethnic Conflict and Civic Life Hindus and Muslims in India*, 6, 7, 106.
15. Varshney *Ethnic Conflict and Civic Life Hindus and Muslims in India*, 6, 7.
16. Varshney *Ethnic Conflict and Civic Life Hindus and Muslims in India*, x.
17. Varshney *Ethnic Conflict and Civic Life Hindus and Muslims in India*, 9.

purpose.[18] He concluded that "the religious violence in India serves the purposes of specific groups, individuals, organizations, and even society as a whole in useful ways that are beneficial to them."[19] Brass hypothesized that if a Hindu political party could enhance its chances in an upcoming election due to a riot, then a manufactured riot would likely occur.[20] Besides politics, underlying causes of these riots and pogroms include disputes between manufacturers and wholesalers, and over land.[21]

Often, riots would be carefully planned and made to appear that Muslims were attacking Hindus and that Hindus were acting in self-defense.[22] The planning included riot rehearsals, initiating actions, and follow-up media interpretations of what happened.[23] Often, these riots would be sponsored and conducted by organized criminal gangs, which only magnified the lethality of the event.[24] Varshney concluded that, "In all violent cities in this project, a nexus of politicians and criminal was evident. Without the involvement of organized gangs, large-scale rioting and tens and hundreds of killings are most unlikely."[25]

The Hindu-Muslim rioting began to rise in the 1960s and peaked in the 1990s.[26] Between 1990-1993, India went through its worst phase of Hindu-Muslim violence since the 1947 partition of India that created Muslim Pakistan.[27] The religious violence climaxed with the planned destruction of the Babri Mosque in Ayodhya, India, on December 6, 1992. Hindus believed this Mosque was built on top of the Hindu God Lord Rama's birthplace – and, as such, was sacrilegious.

From 1989, *Hindutva* campaigns were conducted around India regarding replacing this Mosque with the Rama Mandir temple. On the morning of December 6, 1992, over two hundred thousand volunteers (called *kar sevaks*) arrived at the site and began systematically demolishing the Babri Mosque that afternoon. The next day, a *Hindutva*-organized, nationwide

18. Brass, *The Production of Hindu-Muslim Violence in Contemporary India*, 24.
19. Brass, *The Production of Hindu-Muslim Violence in Contemporary India*, 23.
20. Brass, *The Production of Hindu-Muslim Violence in Contemporary India*, 21.
21. Brass, *The Production of Hindu-Muslim Violence in Contemporary India*, 18.
22. Brass, *The Production of Hindu-Muslim Violence in Contemporary India*, 13, 14.
23. Brass, *The Production of Hindu-Muslim Violence in Contemporary India*, 15.
24. Varshney, *Ethnic Conflict and Civic Life Hindus and Muslims in India*, 11, 47.
25. Varshney, *Ethnic Conflict and Civic Life Hindus and Muslims in India*, 11, 47.
26. Varshney, *Ethnic Conflict and Civic Life Hindus and Muslims in India*, 95, 96.
27. Varshney, *Ethnic Conflict and Civic Life Hindus and Muslims in India*, 53.

pogrom against Muslims and Christians began. Referred to simply as riots in the national media, Muslim and Christian communities across India were viciously attacked, with several thousand people being killed over the next four months.[28]

Hinduism vs. Christianity

Hindus were not only threatened by the increase in Muslims in India, but also by the perceived increase in the number of Christians.[29] However, the percent of Christians in India has been slowly *dropping*, from 2.5 percent in 1971 to 2.3 percent in 2011 (last census result; equals twenty-three million people). Despite the relatively small number of Christians in India (a country of over 1.3 billion people), the BJP declared that faiths other than Hinduism are threats that must be removed.

Taking another approach, Chad Bauman, a professor of religion at Butler University, believes that Hindus perceived Christians as serving as a proxy for globalization in India after the early 1990s. As such, it appeared that the economic disparity gap was growing in favor of Christians, which engendered jealousy and anger among Hindus.[30] As such, Christians are perceived as a severe threat to Hinduism in India.[31]

Anti-Christian violence in India increased dramatically following the general elections in March 1998. The BJP, running on its *Hindutva* platform, won the majority of the 62% turnout and had its leader Atal Vajpayee elected as prime minister. After this election, there was a sharp surge in acts of violence against Christians—led by the RSS.[32] The acts of violence included the burning of churches, physical attacks, sexual assaults, and the destruction of Christian schools, colleges, and even cemeteries.[33]

The attacks against Christians culminated on Christmas Eve 2007 with an outbreak of violence in a village in the Kandhamal district of the State of Orrisa (on the East Coast of India). Groups of Hindus affiliated with RSS burned down over one hundred churches and Christian institutions while

---

28. Sweetman and Malik, eds., *Hinduism in India*, 112–116.
29. Bauman, "Hindu-Christian Conflict in India," 638.
30. Bauman, "Hindu-Christian Conflict in India," 634.
31. Bauman, "Hindu-Christian Conflict in India," 639.
32. Bauman, "Hindu-Christian Conflict in India," 634.
33. Bauman, "Hindu-Christian Conflict in India," 634.

killing as many as fifty Christians.³⁴ Then, in August 2008, an influential Hindu leader was murdered in this State, allegedly by a Christian—but this was not proven. In retaliation for this killing of a Hindu, RSS-affiliated groups proceeded to burn down close to four thousand Christian homes and close to four hundred churches while killing at least forty people, mostly Christians. This resulted in seventy-five thousand people being left homeless.³⁵

The *Arya Samaj*, an old, monotheistic Indian Hindu reform movement, conducted campaigns of mass "purification" to reconvert converts to Christianity and Islam back to Hinduism and to purify members of the lower castes.³⁶ The *Samaj* has been pro-nationalist since its beginning in 1875, and has been intolerant and even militant towards both Christians and Muslims. The RSS has been trying to ally itself with the *Arya Samaj* for decades, even though both organizations have differing visions for India. However, despite the differences, the RSS and *Samaj* have recently been sharing events as well as mutual posts on social media, including discussions about *Hindutva*.³⁷ The RSS has now effectively co-opted the *Arya Samaj* and using this alliance to persecute Christians and Muslims in India even further.

After the BJP won a majority of parliament seats in the April-May 2014 general election, Narendra Modi was elected to be prime minister. Multiple news organizations soon began reporting an increase of violent incidents by Hindus against Christians in India.³⁸ According to the *All India Christian Council*, there was an attack on Christians recorded every forty hours in 2016.³⁹ In a report by the Indian organization *Persecution Relief*, the crimes against Christians increased by 60% from 2016 to 2019. The organization reported a direct link between BJP gaining power in a state and an increase in the attacks against Christians in the country.⁴⁰

34. Bauman, "Hindu-Christian Conflict in India," 634.
35. Bauman, "Hindu-Christian Conflict in India," 634.
36. Bauman, "Hindu-Christian Conflict in India," 639.
37. Punia, "The RSS's Endeavor to Subsume the Arya Samaj is Reaching Fruition," https://caravanmagazine.in/politics/rss-attempt-takeover-arya-samaj-english
38. Kumar, "Violent Persecution of Christians Rises in India," https://www.christianpost.com/news/violent-persecution-christians-india-attack-every-40-hours-report-182039/
39. Kumar, "Violent Persecution of Christians Rises in India," https://www.christianpost.com/news/violent-persecution-christians-india-attack-every-40-hours-report-182039/
40. Mathew, "On Narenda Modi's Watch, Steep Rise in Crime Against Christians Between 2016 and 2019," https://www.nationalheraldindia.com/

Buddhism vs. Islam

Buddhism spread throughout Asia primarily due to trade and missionary efforts. While it was advertised as a peaceful, tranquil set of beliefs, Buddhism also accommodated violence and conflict to protect itself, as well as its monks, monasteries, and adopted countries. Once a kingdom or country adopted Buddhism as its official religion, then Buddhists defended this official position vigorously. Buddhism is currently the official religion in Bhutan, Cambodia, Sri Lanka, Thailand, Myanmar, and Laos (all are Southeast Asian countries).

In Southeast Asia, Buddhists have persecuted Muslims for decades, particularly in Sri Lanka, Thailand, and Myanmar. These countries practice the *Theravada* tradition of Buddhism. Over time, *Theravada* Buddhism in these countries morphed into a militant, ultra-nationalist religion due to the perceived growing Muslim threat in their countries.[41] Military and other security forces have been working out of Buddhist monasteries in these countries. Buddhists feel more protected by the presence of soldiers and police in their monasteries; however, their presence was perceived as a threat by local Muslim residents.[42] In Thailand's southern states, the Thai army even trained civilian militias to protect monasteries and accompany Buddhist monks whenever they left their temples. These actions only heightened the perceived threat posed by Buddhists to local Muslims and further alienating them from the country.[43]

Turning to Islam, it has been making in-roads into Southeast Asia (SEA) since the 7th century CE. The expansion of trade in Asia helped spread Islam as Muslim traders brought it to the region. Sufi missionaries (i.e., Muslim mystics) also played a significant role in spreading the faith by mixing Islamic ideas with existing local beliefs (aka syncretism). Finally, the ruling classes embraced Islam which further aided its permeation throughout SEA.

Today, Sunni Islam is the most practiced religion in Southeast Asia, with over two hundred and forty-two million adherents (over 42% of

---

india/on-narendra-modi-watch-steep-rise-in-crime-against-christians-between-2016-and-2019

41. Lehr, *Militant Buddhism*, 2.

42. Beech, "Buddhists Go to Battle: When Nationalism Overrides Pacifism," https://www.nytimes.com/2019/07/08/world/asia/buddhism-militant-rise.html

43. Lehr, *Militant Buddhism*, 35.

the entire population) *and growing*. PEW Research Center projects that by 2060, India will contain over three hundred and thirty-three million Muslims.[44] There are more Muslims in SEA than any other region in the world, including the Middle East—where Islam originated. On the other hand, Buddhism is practiced by around two hundred and five million people in SEA (around 38% of the total population) and stagnating. On a macro level, one can see the source of conflict as Islam becomes increasingly prevalent while Buddhism struggles to remain the official religion in most SEA countries.

While there are relatively few Muslims in Japan and Korea, there is a sizeable number in China going back close to two thousand years, primarily in the far west in the Central Asia region along the Silk Road trade route. China's Xinjiang Uyghur Autonomous Region (aka Xinjiang) borders eight countries (most of which have a majority of Muslim citizens). It has around twelve million Uyghurs, who are primarily Sunni Muslims, living there (less than half the total population). They are among the oldest Turkic-speaking population in Central Asia. Many historians trace the ancestry of the Uyghur tribe to the Tiele people who lived in the valleys south of Lake Baikal and around the Yenisei River since 357 CE.[45] Despite Xinjiang being mostly desert, it produces a fifth of the world's cotton, and has proven substantial oil and natural gas deposits. Uyghurs are forced to pick cotton and make wool in local textile factories.[46] The Xinjiang Region also accounts for 71 percent of the global photovoltaic solar module production. "Nearly every silicon-based solar module — at least 95 percent of the market — is likely to have some Xinjiang silicon," Jenny Chase, the head of solar analysis at BloombergNEF, told *Politico*.[47] This situation poses an ethical dilemma for Western democracies around the world trying to combat climate change.

In the 1950s, the Chinese Communist Party began moving large numbers of ethnic Han people to this region likely to make it more Chinese. The influx of Han people became even more pronounced after 1990. By the late 20th century, the Han constituted two-fifths of Xinjiang's total population.

44. https://www.pewresearch.org/fact-tank/2019/04/01/the-countries-with-the-10-largest-christian-populations-and-the-10-largest-muslim-populations/

45. Duan, *Dingling, Gaoju and Tiele*, 325–26.

46. https://www.bbc.co.uk/news/extra/nz0g306v8c/china-tainted-cotton

47. https://foreignpolicy.com/2021/04/12/clean-energy-china-xinjiang-uyghur-labor/?utm_source=PostUp&utm_medium=email&utm_campaign=32143&utm_term=Editors%20Picks%20OC&tpcc=32143

Most Han migrants settled in the north of the region, while the Uyghur population centers were resident in the south.[48] Naturally, over time, the economic disparities and ethnic and religious tensions grew between the Uyghur and Han populations. Remember that the Uyghurs are Sunni Muslims and the Han are Communists first, but they may also be adherents to either *Mahayana* Buddhism or Daoism. Social protests led the Chinese government to consider this area a source of terrorism, which became more pronounced following the 9/11 attack terrorist attacks on the United States by the Muslim terrorist group al-Qaeda.

In Xinjiang, a violent outbreak occurred in July 2009, when nearly two hundred people (mostly Han) were killed and over one thousand and seven hundred were injured. Chinese authorities responded by cracking down on Uyghurs, including shootings, arrests, and long jail sentences. Since May 2014, the Chinese government has waged what it calls the "Strike Hard Campaign against Violent Terrorism" program. Xinjiang authorities sent two hundred thousand officials from government agencies, state-owned enterprises, and public institutions to be stationed in villages to monitor and subject them to political propaganda. In August 2016, Communist Party Secretary Chen, Quan-quo, was transferred from Tibet to Xinjiang that resulted in repression reaching new heights starting in 2017.[49]

In 2021, the United Nations reported that 1.5 million Uyghurs and other Muslims had been rounded up and placed into detention or internment camps for rehabilitating since 2018, making them the largest such internment camps in the world since World War II.[50] Of course, there is no Chinese law that allows for such internment or detention camps. There have been numerous reports of maltreatment, overcrowding, torture, and even death occurring in these camps. The detainees are forced to learn Mandarin Chinese, Communist propaganda, and rules applicable to Turkic Muslims, particularly the restricting of the practice of Islam. In January 2021, the U.S. State Department declared that "the Chinese government is committing genocide and crimes against humanity through its wide-scale repression of Uyghurs and other predominantly Muslim ethnic minorities in its northwestern region of Xinjiang, including in its use of

48. Roberts, "The Roots of Cultural Genocide in Xinjiang," https://www.foreignaffairs.com/articles/china/2021-02-10/roots-cultural-genocide-xinjiang

49. Wang, "Eradicating Ideological Viruses," https://www.hrw.org/report/2018/09/09/eradicating-ideological-viruses/chinas-campaign-repression-against-xinjiangs

50. https://www.npr.org/2021/06/10/1005263835/new-report-details-firsthand-accounts-of-torture-from-uyghur-muslims-in-china?ft=nprml&f=1005263835

internment camps and forced sterilization."[51] According to Amnesty International, the Chinese government's actions against the Uyghurs constitutes a crime against humanity, to include an extensive cover-up by the Chinese leadership.[52]

The Chinese government has even requested other countries forcibly return any of their Uyghur citizens to China. According to Maya Wang, a China Senior Researcher for Human Rights Watch, the human rights violations in Xinjiang today are of a scope and scale not seen in China since the 1966-1976 Cultural Revolution.[53] Finally, Sean Roberts, a professor of international affairs at George Washington University, concluded that "Under the guise of counterterrorism, China ramped up its suppression of dissent and repression of religion in the Uyghur homeland. It simultaneously furthered its goals of colonization by investing billions in building new infrastructure and industry in Xinjiang, in the process attracting more Han migrants to the region."[54]

Buddhism vs. Christianity

Buddhism and Christianity are similar in that both advocate for peace and non-violence. However, both religions are responsible for large losses of life over the centuries. For example, the Christian Crusades resulted in the deaths of as many as nine million people from 1095 to 1291 CE.[55] Christianity created a human representative of God on earth to replace Jesus, an elected bishop referred to as the pope. Popes collaborated with monarchical rulers across Europe to form a powerful force against those who would challenge the church. As well, popes authorized Christian Crusades to recover the holy land in the Middle East from Muslim control, among other

---

51. Wong and Buckley, "U.S. Says China's Repression of Uighurs Is 'Genocide,'" https://www.nytimes.com/2021/01/19/us/politics/trump-china-xinjiang.html

52. Wong and Buckley, "U.S. Says China's Repression of Uighurs Is 'Genocide,'" https://www.nytimes.com/2021/01/19/us/politics/trump-china-xinjiang.html

53. Wang, "Eradicating Ideological Viruses," https://www.hrw.org/report/2018/09/09/eradicating-ideological-viruses/chinas-campaign-repression-against-xinjiangs

54. Roberts, "The Roots of Cultural Genocide in Xinjiang," https://www.foreignaffairs.com/articles/china/2021-02-10/roots-cultural-genocide-xinjiang

55. Robertson, *A Short History of Christianity*, 278.

purposes.[56] Buddhists were not as organized as Christians, therefore, had no mechanism such as the Vatican to proselytize by force.

Saint Augustine Hippo developed Just War theory around 386 CE to ensure wars in Europe were morally justifiable using two different criteria: *Jus ad Bellum* (right to go to war) and *Jus in Bello* (right conduct in war). Just War theory postulates that war is *not* always the worst option given essential state responsibilities, potential undesirable outcomes, or preventable atrocities![57] The early Buddhist position on conflict and violence comes close to this early Christian position.[58] Buddhists began to accept a variety of "just war" theories that evolved during the reign of Emperor Ashoka.[59] As well, where Crusaders fought to have their sins forgiven, warrior monks could earn more merit defending the faith than losing merits for killing another person. While Christian noblemen were able to pay the church to have sins forgiven, Buddhists could also provide funding to monasteries or build temples to gain merit to enhance the conditions of their reincarnation.[60]

Following the Korean War (1950-1953), Christianity expanded its influence in South Korea to become one of its national religions. Christians inspired Korean Buddhists to become actively engaged in modern social services, such as supporting hospitals and prisons.[61] This coexistence of Buddhism and Christianity in South Korea is analogous to the coexistence of Buddhism and Shinto in Japan.

Shinto vs. Christianity

Religions can be co-opted by a ruling government to serve its political needs. This co-opting happened during the 20th century, first in Japan and then in Germany. Emperor Hirohito and Imperial Japan hijacked Shinto to control shrine finances and priests beginning around 1900. Called "State Shinto" by U.S. military leaders at the end of World War II, Shinto was modified by Imperial Japan to reflect a nationalist ideology with the

---

56. Reference *Killing for God* by Stephen Schwalbe published by Lexington Books on July 15, 2020.
57. Guthrie and Quinlan, *Just War: The Just War Tradition*, 11–15.
58. Tikhonov and Brekke, eds., *Buddhism and Violence*, 6.
59. Tikhonov and Brekke, eds., *Buddhism and Violence*, 9.
60. Roy, *Hinduism and the Ethics of Warfare in South Asia*, 54.
61. Tikhonov and Brekke, eds., *Buddhism and Violence*, 56.

emperor considered a divine being. Worship at any Shinto shrine (including the several hundred built in Korea) was considered an act of patriotism and loyalty to the emperor. Shinto shrines were also for prayer for those killed in combat.[62]

In Germany, Adolph Hitler, brought up as a Catholic, approved a Christian derivative religion called *Positive Christianity* (Negative Christianity was associated with Protestantism). This form of Christianity was intended to demonstrate Hitler's and Nazi belief in Christianity to co-opt the German population, wary that the Nazis were really atheists. After all, Germany had been a Christian state for over 1,000 years by this time. Positive Christianity became a mixture of Nazi ideology and Christian faith, involving replacing the Bible with *Mein Kampf* and the Christian Cross with the Nazi Swastika.[63] Savarkar, the creator of *Hindutva*, drew parallels between Germans and Hindus regarding Jews and Muslims, respectively.[64] Muslims were often portrayed as a cancer in society that needed to be removed.[65]

Fundamentalist Conflict

Finally, fundamentalist movements in some religions have led to conflict. Religious fundamentalism can be defined as the belief in the absolute authority of sacred scripture or in the teachings of a spiritual leader, prophet, or god. It is a natural reaction to changes incurred by modernization. Fundamentalists tend to reject most aspects of modernity, especially religious pluralism and secularism (i.e., separation of church and state).[66]

---

62. Victoria, *Zen at War*, 98.

63. Shirer, The Rise and Fall of the Third Reich, 240.

64. Punia "The RSS's Endeavor to Subsume the Arya Samaj is Reaching Fruition," https://caravanmagazine.in/politics/rss-attempt-takeover-arya-samaj-english; Roychowdhury, "Vinayak Damodar Savarkar: He admired Hitler and other lesser-known facts about him,"
https://indianexpress.com/article/research/vinayak-damodar-savarkar-135th-birth-anniversary-he-admired-hitler-and-other-lesser-known-facts-about-him-5194470/

65. Von de Waals, *The Rohingya in Myanmar*, 15.

66. Schwalbe, *Killing for God*, 9–10.

Islamic Fundamentalism

Islamic fundamentalism began to evolve in the twentieth century and has been expanding ever since. It is based strictly on the *Qur'an* and Hadith (i.e., the sayings and customs of the Prophet Muhammad). According to religious scholars, such as Scott Appleby, a professor of history at the University of Notre Dame, and Michael Cook, a professor of Near Eastern Studies at Princeton University, fundamentalism is most prevalent within Islam as a reaction to modernization and Westernization.[67] The most fundamentalist sect of Islam today is *Wahhabism*, the national religion of the Kingdom of Saudi Arabia. Imam Wahhab (1703–1792 CE) was a religious leader in southern Arabia who sought to return Islam to the "golden age" of the Prophet Muhammad. Wahhab joined with Muhammad bin Saud in 1744 to create Saudi Arabia, where Wahhab was responsible for religious matters, and Saud was responsible for political and military matters.[68] *Wahhabism* is the common Islamic tradition of most Muslim extremist groups, including al-Qaeda.

Hindu Fundamentalism

In Hinduism, fundamentalism took the form of *Hindutva*, which started at the end of the 19th century, formalized by Savarkar in 1923, and has become prominent in India today. As noted previously, *Hindutva* is represented in the Indian national government by the Bharatiya Janata Party ("Indian People's Party"—BJP) and culturally by the Rashtriya Swayamsevak Sangh ("National Volunteer Core"—RSS).[69] *Hindutva* has been described as "Hinduism on steroids."[70]

The most important factor motivating *Hindutva* is that while Hindus were (and still are) the majority population in India, Muslims of the Delhi Sultanate, followed by the Mughal Empire, ruled the country from 1206 CE until the British Raj took control in 1858. Finally, India became an independent country run by Hindus in 1947, after over seven hundred and

---

67. Almond, Appleby, and Sivan, *Strong Religion*, 104; Cook, *Ancient Religions, Modern Politics*, 441.
68. Schwalbe, *Killing for God*, 13–14.
69. Sharma, "On Hindu, Hindustan, Hinduism and Hindutva," 43.
70. Sharma, "On Hindu, Hindustan, Hinduism and Hindutva," 43.

forty years of foreign rule.⁷¹ Ameya Singh, a Ph.D. candidate in area studies at Oxford University, described *Hindutva* as,

> Hindutva is therefore better understood as the politically-motivated reification of Hindu culture in nation-state terms. At the turn of the 20th century, founding members of the Hindutva proper valorized the *racial superiority of Hindu peoples* in order to tap into the darker recesses of their collective unconscious and infuse the Indian anti-colonial nationalist struggle with a militant and martial zeal.⁷²

Finally, Arvind Sharma, a professor of comparative religion at McGill University, concluded that "The militant tradition is also seen by *Hindutva* historians as a continuation of the militant tradition found in Hinduism in former times."⁷³

In January 2021, *India Today—Karvy Insights* conducted a "Mood of the Nation" poll of over twelve thousand Indians throughout India to determine the status of *Hindutva*. The poll results showed that backing for the RSS *Hindutva* agenda was "solid"; support for Prime Minister Narenda Modi and his brand of national-populism was "scaling stratospheric heights"; and Modi's government's performance received a "big thumbs up."⁷⁴ The brand of national-populism that Prime Minister Modi initiated transcended caste barriers in defense of Hindus against the perceived growing Muslim threat. This approach was magnified by the fact that Modi came from a caste classified as just above Dalits, the former untouchables.⁷⁵ On the other hand, the communal violence in India's major cities has left a mark on Modi's legacy. During the sectarian riots in 2002 that saw over two thousand people killed (mostly Muslims), Modi was the Chief Minister (similar to an American governor) of the State of Gujarat where the riots occurred. Modi was even banned from visiting the United States—until he

---

71. Sharma, "On Hindu, Hindustan, Hinduism and Hindutva," 45.

72. Singh, "Hindutva's Realism in Modi's Foreign Policy," https://thediplomat.com/2021/01/hindutvas-realism-in-modis-foreign-policy/

73. Sharma, "On Hindu, Hindustan, Hinduism and Hindutva," 45.

74. Chengappa, "Mood of the Nation Poll: High Tide of Hindutva," https://www.indiatoday.in/magazine/cover-story/story/20210201-high-tide-of-hindutva-1761592-2021-01-22

75. Jaffrelot, "Rise of Hindutva has Enabled a Counter-revolution Against Mandal's Gains," https://indianexpress.com/article/opinion/columns/hindu-nationalism-mandal-commission-upper-caste-politics-modi-govt-7181746/; Sharma, "On Hindu, Hindustan, Hinduism and Hindutva," 46.

became prime minister in 2014. Despite all of this, most Indians support the *Hindutva* efforts by the government, including the construction of the new Ram temple in Ayodhya (previously discussed), the revocation of Article 370 in Kashmir, and the passing of the Citizenship Amendment Bill.

Kashmir, located in the very northern portion of India, is a mountainous Himalayan area that both India and Pakistan lay claim to and even went to war over. Article 370 of India's constitution allowed the Kashmir state additional autonomy, including its own constitution, flag, and ability to make laws. This law was in place for seventy years until Prime Minister Modi's government suddenly revoked it in late 2019 as it was part of his party's election platform. Modi wanted Kashmir to be on the same footing as the rest of India, which would allow for outside investment in the state, potentially making it more Hindu and less Muslim.[76]

As for the Citizenship Amendment Bill (CAB), it was passed by Parliament and enacted into law in December 2019. The CAB amended the 64-year-old Indian Citizenship law, which prohibited illegal immigrants from becoming Indian citizens. The CAB offers amnesty to *non-Muslim* illegal immigrants from neighboring countries fleeing religious persecution. However, where the CAB identifies six religious minority communities that qualify for amnesty (i.e., Hindu, Sikh, Buddhist, Jain, Parsi, and Christian), it notably leaves out Muslims (of which there are over 195 million in India). Coincidentally, there are millions of Muslims being persecuted in India's neighboring countries today, including the Rohingyas in Myanmar and the Ahmadis in Pakistan. The CAB also violates the secular principles in the Indian Constitution, including preventing faith from being a condition of citizenship. However, the Indian Constitution also provides ample grounds for the state to interfere in religious affairs.[77] It appears that though the CAB is directed at foreigners, its primary purpose is to delegitimize Muslim citizenship in India. This bill has already prompted widespread protests in the northeastern part of the county bordering Bangladesh.[78]

---

76. https://www.bbc.com/news/world-asia-india-49234708

77. Vaishnav, "Religious Nationalism and India's Future," https://carnegieendowment.org/2019/04/04/religious-nationalism-and-india-s-future-pub-78703

78. https://www.bbc.com/news/world-asia-india-50670393

Conclusion

In conclusion, the comparison of conflict among various religious combinations of the Asian and Abrahamic religions revealed a few key points. First, the more structured religions, such as Islam and Christianity, were more successful in proselytizing than the Asian religions. Islam initially replaced Hinduism in India and is currently challenging Buddhism in Southeast Asia. Note that there are more Muslims in the world today (around two billion) than Hindus (around one billion) and Buddhists (around a half billion)—combined.

Second, Christianity has much in common with Buddhism philosophically and historically. Both religions focus philosophically on peace while, in reality, facilitating killing on a large scale (e.g., Crusades in Europe and Buddhist self-preservation in Southeast Asia, respectively).

Third, Christianity also has something in common with Shinto in that both religions were co-opted by dictators (Hitler and Hirohito, respectively) to enhance national war efforts during World War II.

Lastly, both Islam and Hinduism witnessed conflict due to fundamentalism as a reaction to change and modernization. The conflict resulting from both Islamic and Hindu fundamentalism is on-going around the world today.

In summary, according to Gier, Islam and Christianity have worse records of religious violence than Hinduism and Buddhism around the world.[79]

---

79. Gier, *The Origins of Religious Violence*, xi.

CHAPTER 11

Conclusion

IN SUMMARY, IN THIS book, we discussed the three main religions of Asia – Hinduism in India, Buddhism in China and Southeast Asia, and Shinto in Japan. Then, we compared them with two of the Abrahamic religions – Islam and Christianity. We determined that Hinduism accommodates violence and conflict (much as Islam does). For example, there are two sacred epics about war—*Mahabharata* and the *Ramayana*, where the *Mahabharata* War was an intra-Aryan war, while the *Ramayana* War was against non-Aryans.

While Buddhism evolved from Hinduism, it cast a pacifist influence on it. Many Hindu scholars, including Savarkar, believe this Buddhist pacifism was one reason Hinduism was defeated by Islam. In fact, Islam began to spread into India as early as the 7th century CE, eventually encompassing the entire South Asian peninsula for over 600 years.

Today, religious intolerance is at an all-time high in India with its gradual adoption of *Hindutva*, a nationalist version of Hinduism that resembled and even had connections with fascist Germany and Italy of the early 20th century. Now, India ranks as one of the world's worst countries regarding religious intolerance, especially regarding Muslims and Christians. The bottom line is that India's intercommunal religious conflict is likely to continue for the foreseeable future. However, as bad as Hinduism has been over the centuries, Buddhism, even with its pacifism, accommodates and facilitates conflict and violence more than Hinduism.

Buddhism historically has been perceived as a peaceful and tranquil religion with its fundamental tenet of *ahisma* (i.e., non-violence). However, there are differences regarding the justification for violence in the two primary Buddhist traditions, *Theravada* and *Mahayana*. *Theravada* Buddhism only allows for violence in defense of Buddhism, while the *Mahayana* tradition justifies the use of violence to either eliminate conflict or to save another person's life. In any case, all Buddhist traditions have had military monks. Buddhist military monks are justified in killing if their *intention* is to protect either Buddhism itself or the nation that has embraced it. Violence and conflict became common with Buddhism once it became affiliated with state governments. Today, Buddhist leaders in the continental Southeast Asian countries have the perception that Buddhism itself is under attack by the growing Muslim communities in the region. Buddhist scholars have declared that once a race or religion is extinguished, it can never be restored. Therefore, the Buddhist conflict with Muslims in SEA, such as in Myanmar, is characterized as existential.

Japan's Shinto also has the common perception of being a peaceful and serene religion. However, it began to evolve into a military religion with the Meiji Empire Restoration in 1868 CE. It was transformed into State Shinto leading up to and including World War II, where all religions in Japan were required to revere the emperor as a divine human and support the nation's war efforts. For example, Buddhist priests and monks were drafted into the military or forced to become manual laborers. The bottom line is that State Shinto was created to suppress the political power of Shrine Shinto and Buddhism in Japan while increasing the power of the Meiji regime.

When comparing Abrahamic and Asian religions regarding violence and conflict, one is struck by the many similarities between Islam and Hinduism/Buddhism, and between Christianity and Shinto. Beginning with Islam and Hinduism, both the scriptures of Hinduism and Islam readily accommodate violence, reflecting their respective civilization's long histories of conflict (part of the Hindu and Arab cultures, respectively). The primary difference between Hinduism and Islam regarding conflict is that Hinduism does not seek to proselytize beyond South Asia while Islam has a goal of world domination (*Dar al-Harb*).

Regarding Islam and Buddhism, the Muslim population's growth in Southeast Asia is perceived as a significant threat to the Buddhist regimes running the many countries in this region of the world. There are now more Muslims in SEA than any other region in the world. Once a kingdom or country adopts Buddhism as its official religion, then Buddhists defend this official position vigorously. This perceived threat from Muslims has

CONCLUSION

resulted in changes in the Buddhist *Theravada* tradition in this region to become more militant and ultra-nationalist. An example of this more militant *Theravada* Buddhism can be found with the 969 Movement in Myanmar dedicated to forcibly removing Muslims from the country.

Shinto and Christianity only have the militarization of their respective religions before and during World War II in common. In the 19th century, the militarization of Shinto began to take root, evolving to become State Shinto, while Hitler created Positive Christianity prior to World War II. In both cases, religion was used to co-opt the support of their respective populations and secure the assets of the respective religions to help in the war effort. There is no current militant version of Shinto or Christianity today.

It appears that religions worldwide have been the source of violence and conflict since history began to be recorded. Moreover, this religious violence usually did not occur until after a religion aligned with a ruling government, thereby bestowing the ruler or government divine authority. Given the nature of humans, this trend of merging religion with politics is likely to continue for the foreseeable future. The main conclusion of the 2020 book, *Killing for God*, was that "religious conflict appears to have served humankind's political purposes more than to serve any of these [Abrahamic] religions' conceptions of God or Allah. With that in mind, humankind could strive to remove religion from politics, and remove the religious aspect of conflict in the world to more readily come to compromise and peace."[1] In the case of the Abrahamic religions, the motivation for people to fight was to have their sins forgiven so they might go to Heaven. In the case of the Asian religions, the motivation was to gain more merits than demerits to improve their reincarnation potential.

This book discussed how governments seized control of religions and modified them to support the state. The best example of this was when Imperial Japan modified Shinto to create State Shinto to support the war effort, with the emperor being considered a human god. The current example of this is India's modification of Hinduism into *Hindutva* to legitimize India's cleansing itself of foreign religions like Islam. As such, India has morphed into an illiberal theocracy where democratic institutions, such as the constitution and domestic laws, are subjugated to *Hindutva* policies. Theocratic governments, such as those found in India and Iran, facilitate

---

1. Schwalbe, *Killing for God*, 133.

religious conflict, hence, are a continuing threat to world peace. In the two thousand and five hundred years of Buddhism, no ruler or government ever hijacked this religion to support its war effort.

To bring the insights of this book into some sense of the real world today, let's imagine a scenario where the U.S. military forces are tasked with an interdiction operation to prevent the genocide of the Rohingya people in Myanmar. American military targeters may have been trained *not* to consider religious or cultural facilities as potential military targets based on the 1907 Hague Convention. This Convention requires parties to an armed conflict to take "all necessary steps" for the protection of "buildings dedicated to religion, art, science or charitable purposes, historic monuments, hospitals and places where the sick and wounded are collected, *provided they are not being used at the time for military purposes*."[2] However, as we have discussed, Buddhist monasteries in SEA (including Myanmar) have been used as military headquarters, weapon storage facilities, and even prisoner of war detention centers. Knowing Asian religious background such as this would allow U.S. military operations in this part of the world to be more efficient and effective and not mistakenly self-handicapped.

Another key aspect of religious conflict that we discussed was the motivation due to differences in religious beliefs. It is human nature to believe that one's own values are correct and do not need changing. Values are the foundation of religion; hence, when values are different among religions, this causes friction—potentially leading to violence and conflict. As there are many different cultures around the world, and as most religions are proselytized, they adopt some of the local beliefs and become syncretic. Historically, we have witnessed conflicts between and even within various religions around the world due to these differences.

Instead of being threatened by differing values, we should embrace them. The world would be rather dull if the only culture and values in it were White Anglo-Saxon Protestant, as an example. The Unitarian Universalist Church (UUC) and the Universal Life Church (ULC) both exist to recognize and cherish the differences in all religions. The UUC believes that one can increase appreciation for intellectual freedom and inclusive love from these various religions. Its members seek inspiration and derive insights from all major world religions.[3] The ULC believes that universal

---

2. https://www.loc.gov/law/help/us-treaties/bevans/m-ust000001-0631.pdf
3. Visit https://www.uuchurch.org/

Conclusion

beliefs interconnect all religions, and that each religion therefore contains valid aspects.[4]

Finally, it is also human nature to want to live. The same urge exists within religions as well. Whenever the leaders of a religion feel their religion is threatened with replacement by another religion within a country or region, then it is natural to want to counter this threat. We are seeing this first-hand in continental Southeast Asia with Islam threatening to replace Buddhism—as it replaced Hinduism in India for over 600 years. As a result, Muslims are being attacked on a regular basis across numerous SEA countries as their numbers grow and the number of Buddhists diminishes. Buddhist leaders are effectively able to rally Buddhist support using this perceived threat.

Something in common regarding all religions in the world is that they emanate from people with self-proclaimed divine inspiration, more often than not for self-enrichment or self-promotion. Any person in the past could have started a religion (e.g., Jim Jones, David Koresh, et al.), but other than their word, there is nothing (i.e., no tangible evidence) to link them to a supreme deity. People follow such charismatic leaders based *purely on faith*. This religious faith is not a valid justification for violence and conflict.

The bottom line is that Christianity and Islam have worse records of religious violence and conflict throughout history than Hinduism and Buddhism. This is likely due to the Abrahamic religions being more organized, structured, and integrated with government.

---

4. Visit https://www.themonastery.org/

About the Author

Stephen Schwalbe is an adjunct professor at Columbia College. Formerly, he was a professor at the Air War College and American Public University. During his thirty-four-year career in the U.S. Air Force, he served as the Assistant Defense Intelligence Officer for the Middle East and Terrorism, Air Attaché to South Korea, Air Attaché to Jordan, and Inspection Director for the Department of Defense Inspector General.

Bibliography

Anonymous (the author was a professor in Indian and foreign universities). "Rise of Hindu Fundamentalism," Lausanne Global Analysis, Vol. 8, Issue 3 (May 2019) https://www.lausanne.org/content/lga/2019-05/the-rise-of-hindu-fundamentalism

Albert, Eleanor and Lindsay Maizland. "The Rohingya Crisis," *Council of Foreign Relations* (January 23, 2020) https://www.cfr.org/backgrounder/rohingya-crisis

Almond, Gabriel, Scott Appleby, and Emmanuel Sivan. *Strong Religion*. Chicago: University of Chicago Press, 2003.

Armstrong, Karen. *Fields of Blood*. New York: Alfred Knopf, 2014.

Baird, Ian. "Lao Buddhist Monks Involvement in Political and Military Resistance to the Lao Democratic Republic Government Since 1975," Journal of Asian Studies, Volume 71, Issue 3 (August, 2012) http://journals.cambridge.org/abstract_S002191 1812000642

Barton, David. "Buddhism and Shinto: The Two Pillars of Japanese Culture," *Japanology* (June 20, 2016) https://japanology.org/2016/06/buddhism-and-shinto-the-two-pillars-of-japanese-culture/

De Bary, Theodore. ed. *Sources of Chinese Tradition Volume 1*. New York: Columbia University Press, 1960.

———. *Sources of Japanese Tradition Volume I*. New York: Columbia University Press, 1958.

Bauman, Chad. "Hindu-Christian Conflict in India: Globalization, Conversion, and the Coterminal Castes and Tribes," *The Journal of Asian Studies*, Vol. 72, No. 3 (August 2013) https://www.cambridge.org/core/journals/journal-of-asian-studies/article/abs/hinduchristian-conflict-in-india-globalization-conversion-and-the-coterminal-castes-and-tribes/D609BE169609FD3046542572396DD91C

Baumer, Christopher. *The History of Central Asia: The Age of Islam and the Mongols*. London: Bloomsbury, 2018.

Bechert, Heinz, and Richard Gombrich. (eds.) *The World of Buddhism*. London: Thames and Hudson, 1984.

Becker, Elizabeth. "Buddhism in Laos Adapts to Communist Tenets," *The Washington Post* (May 8, 1979) https://www.washingtonpost.com/archive/politics/1979/05/08/buddhism-in-laos-adapts-to-communist-tenets/90a0feeo-cd99-4290-b688-6bdfb8945f72/

Beech, Hannah. "Buddhists Go to Battle: When Nationalism Overrides Pacifism," *New York Times* (July 8, 2019) https://www.nytimes.com/2019/07/08/world/asia/buddhism-militant-rise.html

Bibliography

Brass, Paul. *The Production of Hindu-Muslim Violence in Contemporary India*. New Delhi: Oxford University Press, 2003.

Brockington, J.L. *The Sanskrit Epics*. Netherlands: Brill, 1998.

Cartwright, Mark. "Buddhism in Ancient Korea," *World History Encyclopedia* (November 15, 2010) https://www.ancient.eu/article/973/buddhism-in-ancient-korea/

Chengappa, Raj. "Mood of the Nation poll: High Tide of Hindutva," *India Today* (January 22, 2021) https://www.indiatoday.in/magazine/cover-story/story/20210201-high-tide-of-hindutva-1761592-2021-01-22

Cook, Michael. *Ancient Religions, Modern Politics*. Princeton: Princeton University Press, 2014.

Cox, Rory. "Expanding the History of the Just War: The Ethics of War in Ancient Egypt," *International Studies Quarterly*, Volume 61, Issue 2 (June 2017) https://academic.oup.com/isq/article-abstract/61/2/371/3865376

Davies, Roger. *Japanese Culture: The Religious and Philosophical Foundations*. Tokyo: Tuttle, 2016.

DeNapoli, Antoinette. "Earning God through the One-Hundred Rupee Note," *Religions*, 9:12 (2018) https://www.mdpi.com/2077-1444/9/12/408

Doniger, Wendy. *On Hinduism*. Oxford: Oxford University Press, 2014.

Duan, Lianqin. *Dingling, Gaoju and Tiele*. Shanghai: Shanghai People's Press, 1988.

Ford, Eugene. *Cold War Monks*. New Haven: Yale University Press, 2017.

Frank, Richard B. *Downfall: The End of the Imperial Japanese Empire*. New York: Penguin, 2001.

Fronsdal, Gil. *The Dhammapada*. Boulder: Shambhala, 2006.

Garon, Sheldon. "State and Religion in Imperial Japan, 1912-1945," *The Journal of Japanese Studies* Vol. 12, No. 2 (Summer, 1986) https://www.jstor.org/stable/132389?seq=1

Gier, Nicholas F. *The Origins of Religious Violence: An Asian Perspective*. Lanham, MD: Lexington, 2014.

Gombrich, Richard F. *How Buddhism Began. The Conditioned Genesis of the Early Teachings*. New Delhi: Munshiram Manoharlal, 1997.

Gopin, Marc. *Between Eden and Armageddon*. Oxford: Oxford University Press, 2000.

Gort, Jerald, Henry Jackson, and Hendrik Vroom. eds. *Religion, Conflict and Reconciliation*. New York: Rodopi, 2002.

Gunasingham, Amresh. "Buddhist Extremism in Sri Lanka and Myanmar," *Counter Terrorist Trends and Analyses*, Vol. 11, No. 3 (March 2019) https://www.jstor.org/stable/pdf/26617827.pdf

Guthrie, Charles and Michael Quinlan. *Just War: The Just War Tradition: Ethics in Modern Warfare*. London: Bloomsbury, 2007.

Hall, John. *Religion and Violence: Social Processes in Comparative Perspective*, https://projects.iq.harvard.edu/files/wcfia/files/569_jhallreligionviolence11-01.pdf

Hardacre, Helen. *Shinto and the State, 1868-1988*. Princeton: Princeton University Press, 1989.

Harvey, Peter. An Introduction to Buddhism: Teachings, History and Practices *(2nd ed.)*. Cambridge, UK: Cambridge University Press, 2013.

———. An Introduction to Buddhist Ethics: Foundations, Values, and Issues. Cambridge, UK: Cambridge University Press, 2000.

Holt, John Clifford. *The Buddhist Viṣṇu: Religious Transformation, Politics, and Culture*. New Delhi: Motilal Banarsidass, 2008.

Bibliography

Huntington, Samuel. *The Clash of Civilization and the Remaking of the World Order.* New York: Simon and Shuster, 1996.

Jaffrelot, Christophe. "Rise of Hindutva has Enabled a Counter-revolution Against Mandal's Gains," *The Indian Express* (April 2, 2021) https://indianexpress.com/article/opinion/columns/hindu-nationalism-mandal-commission-upper-caste-politics-modi-govt-7181746/

Jalon, Allan. "Meditating On War and Guilt, Zen Says It's Sorry," *New York Times* (January 11, 2003) https://www.nytimes.com/2003/01/11/books/meditating-on-war-and-guilt-zen-says-it-s-sorry.html

Jerryson, Michael. *Buddhist Fury.* Oxford: Oxford University Press, 2011.

Jerryson, Michael and Mark Juergensmeyer. eds. *Buddhist Warfare.* Oxford: Oxford University Press, 2010.

Juergensmeyer, Mark, Margo Kitts, and Michael Jerryson. eds. *Violence and the World's Religious Traditions.* Oxford: Oxford University Press, 2017.

Keown, Damien. *Buddhism.* New York: Sterling, 2009.

Keyes, Charles. "Theravada Buddhism and Buddhist Nationalism: Sri Lanka, Myanmar, Cambodia, and Thailand," *The Review of Faith and International Affairs* (December 1, 2016) https://www.tandfonline.com/doi/abs/10.1080/15570274.2016.1248497?journalCode=rfia20

Kitagawa, Joseph. "The Buddhist Transformation in Japan," *History of Religions,* Volume 4, Number 2 (Winter, 1965) https://www.journals.uchicago.edu/doi/abs/10.1086/462509

Kopf, David. *The Brahmo Samaj and the Shaping of the Modern Indian Mind* (Princeton: Princeton University Press, 1973).

Kumar, Anugrah. "Violent Persecution of Christians Rises in India," *Christianpost.com* (April 29, 2017) https://www.christianpost.com/news/violent-persecution-christians-india-attack-every-40-hours-report-182039/

Langley, Myrtle. *World Religions.* Oxford: A Lion Manual, 1993.

Lehr, Peter. *Militant Buddhism.* Switzerland: Palgrave MacMillan, 2019.

Leidig, Eviane. "Hindutva as a Variant of Right-wing Extremism," *Patterns of Prejudice,* 54:3 (July 17, 2020) https://www.tandfonline.com/doi/full/10.1080/0031322X.2020.1759861

Mathew, Ashlin. "On Narenda Modi's Watch, Steep Rise in Crime against Christians between 2016 and 2019," *National Herald* (March 19, 2020) https://www.nationalheraldindia.com/india/on-narendra-modi-watch-steep-rise-in-crime-against-christians-between-2016-and-2019

Nalini, Rangan. *Hinduism.* Broomall, PA: Mason Crest, 2017.

Nelson, John K. *A Year in the Life of a Shinto Shrine.* Seattle: University of Washington Press, 2000.

Olivelle, Patrick. *Upanishads.* Oxford: Oxford University Press, 1996.

Panikkar, Raimon. *Hinduism.* Maryknoll, NY: Orbis, 2016.

Parrinder, Geoffrey. ed. *World Religions.* New York: Hamlyn, 1971.

Phillips, Stephen. *Yoga, Karma, and Rebirth: A Brief History and Philosophy.* New York: Columbia University Press, 2009.

Pillalamarri, Akhilesh. "Buddhism and Islam in Asia: A Long and Complicated History," *The Diplomat,* (October 29, 2017) https://thediplomat.com/2017/10/buddhism-and-islam-in-asia-a-long-and-complicated-history/

Bibliography

Punia, Mandeep. "The RSS's Endeavor to Subsume the Arya Samaj is Reaching Fruition," (June 30, 2019) https://caravanmagazine.in/politics/rss-attempt-takeover-arya-samaj-english

Pyysiainen, Ilkka. "Buddhism, Religion, and the Concept of God," *Numen*, Vol. 50, No. 2 (2003) https://www.jstor.org/stable/3270517?seq=1

Rambachan, Anantanand. "The Coexistence of Violence and Nonviolence in Hinduism," *Journal of Ecumenical Studies*, Vol. 52, No. 1 (Winter, 2017) https://muse.jhu.edu/article/655703/pdf#:~:text=The%20re%2D%20lationship%20between%20violence,Hinduism%20must%20be%20properly%20contextualized.&text=Society%20could%20not%20survive%20without,in%20the%20defense%20of%20dharma

Roberts, Sean. "The Roots of Cultural Genocide in Xinjiang," *Foreign Affairs* (February 10, 2021) https://www.foreignaffairs.com/articles/china/2021-02-10/roots-cultural-genocide-xinjiang

Robertson, John M. *A Short History of Christianity*. London: Watts & Company, 1902.

Rosen, Steven. *Essential Hinduism*. Santa Barbara: Praeger, 2006.

Roy, Kaushik. *Hinduism and the Ethics of Warfare in South Asia*. Cambridge: Cambridge University Press, 2012.

Roychowdhury, Adrija. "Vinayak Damodar Savarkar: He Admired Hitler and Other Lesser-Known Facts about Him," *The Indian Express* (May 28, 2018) https://indianexpress.com/article/research/vinayak-damodar-savarkar-135th-birth-anniversary-he-admired-hitler-and-other-lesser-known-facts-about-him-5194470/

Rummel, R.J. *Statistics of Democide: Chapter 3 – Statistics of Japanese Democide* (New Jersey: Transaction, 1997) https://www.hawaii.edu/powerkills/SOD.CHAP3.HTM#:~:text=From%20the%20invasion%20of%20China,including%20Western%20prisoners%20of%20war

Savarkar, Vinayak. *Essentials of Hindutva*. Independent, 1928.

Schwalbe, Stephen. *Killing for God*. Lanham, MD: Lexington, 2020.

Selengut, Charles. *Sacred Fury*. Walnut Creek, CA: AltaMira, 2003.

Sharma, Arvind. "On Hindu, Hindustan, Hinduism and Hindutva," *Numen*, Vol. 49, No. 1 (2002) https://www.jstor.org/stable/3270470?seq=1

Sheikh, Naveed. *Body Count*. Jordan: The Royal aal al-Bayt Institute for Islamic Thought, 2009. https://rissc.jo/docs/bodycount_final.pdf

Sherwood, Harriet. "Religion: Why Faith is Becoming More and More Popular," https://www.theguardian.com/news/2018/aug/27/religion-why-is-faith-growing-and-what-happens-next

Shinozaki, Michio, Brook Ziporyn, and David Earhart translators. *The Threefold Lotus Sutra* Tokyo: Kosei, 2019.

Shirer, William. *The Rise and Fall of the Third Reich: A History of Nazi Germany*. London: Secker & Warburg, 1960.

Singh, Ameya. "Hindutva's Realism in Modi's Foreign Policy," *The Diplomat* (January 1, 2021) https://thediplomat.com/2021/01/hindutvas-realism-in-modis-foreign-policy/

Skilton, Andrew. *A Concise History of Buddhism*. Birmingham: Windhorse, 1995.

Smith, Huston. *The World's Religions*. San Francisco: Harper, 1991.

Snelling, John. *The Buddhist handbook: A Complete Guide to Buddhist Teaching and Practice*. London: Century, 1987.

Bibliography

Strathern, Alan. "Why are Buddhist Monks Attacking Muslims?" *BBC News* (May 2, 2013) https://www.bbc.com/news/magazine-22356306

Sweetman, Will, and Aditya Malik. eds. *Hinduism in India*. New Delhi: Sage, 2016.

Tahtinen, Unto. *Non-violence as an Ethical Principle*. Finland: Turun Yliopisto, 1964.

Tamashige, Sachiko. "Seeing Where Shinto and Buddhism Cross," *Japan Times* (May 16, 2013) https://www.japantimes.co.jp/culture/2013/05/16/arts/seeing-where-shinto-and-buddhism-cross/

Thero, Walpola Rahula. *The Heritage of Bhikkhu*. New York: Grove, 1974.

Tikhonov, Vladimir, and Torkel Brekke. eds. *Buddhism and Violence*. New York: Routledge, 2013.

Vaishnav, Milan. "Religious Nationalism and India's Future," *Carnegie Endowment for International Peace* (April 4, 2019) https://carnegieendowment.org/2019/04/04/religious-nationalism-and-india-s-future-pub-78703

Varshney, Ashtosh. *Ethnic Conflict and Civic Life Hindus and Muslims in India*. New Haven: Yale University Press, 2002.

Victoria, Brian. *Zen at War*. Lanham, MD: Rowman & Littlefield, 2006.

Von de Waals, Peter. *The Rohingya in Myanmar between displacement and genocide: A Religious war of Buddhism against Islam?* Coppell, TX: Independent, 2020.

Vyasa. Translated by Telang. *The Bhagavad Gita*. Digireads.com, 2017.

Wang, Maya. "Eradicating Ideological Viruses" *Human Rights Watch* (September 9, 2018) https://www.hrw.org/report/2018/09/09/eradicating-ideological-viruses/chinas-campaign-repression-against-xinjiangs

Watson, Burton. *The Zen Teachings of Master Lin-Chi: A Translation of the Lin-Chi Lu*. New York: Columbia University Press, 1999.

Wilson, Jeff. *Mourning the Unborn Dead: A Buddhist Ritual Comes to America*. Oxford, UK: Oxford University Press, 2009.

Wong, Edward and Chris Buckley. "U.S. Says China's Repression of Uighurs Is 'Genocide'" *New York Times* (January 19, 2021) https:wwwnytimes.com/2021/01/19/us/politics/trump-china-xinjiang.html

Index

969 Movement, 91, 143

Adultery, 56, 59
Afghanistan, 30, 76, 94, 121
Ahisma, 11, 55, 80, 141
Ahmadis, 139
Akhand Bharat, 30, 42
Alcohol, 51, 53, 54, 57, 68
Alexandria, 75
All India Christian Council, 130
Allah, 6, 7, 124, 143
Almond, Gabriel, 14, 40, 123
Alms, 50
Amaterasu Omikami, 101
Ambalangoda, 94
Amidism, 69
Amnesty International, 43, 134
Anatman, 58, 113
Ancestor, 61, 98, 101
    Veneration, 61, 114
    Worship, 61
Apostle Paul, 29, 75, 114
Appleby, Scott, 137
Arabic, 7
Arhat, 66, 80
Arinori, Mori, 107
Aristotle, 12
Arjuna, 25, 26, 38
Armstrong, Karen, 12
Article 36, 122
Article 370, 42, 138–9
Aryan, 17, 37, 71, 141
Arya Samaj, 31, 117, 123, 130,
Ashoka, Emperor, 50, 65, 74–5, 135
Athens, 75
Atman, 19, 113

Augustine, Saint, 12, 135
Avatar, 24, 26, 113
Ayodhya, India, 42, 123, 128, 138

Babri Masjid, 42
Babri Mosque, 42, 127
Badrinath, India, 124
Baekje Kingdom, 76, 102
Bangladesh, 30–1, 42, 65, 139
Baqi, Mir, 42
De Bary, Theodore, 119
Basu, Chandranath, 28
Battle, 12, 14, 25–6, 37, 39
Battle of Yorktown, 37
Bauman, Chad, 129
Bechert, Heinz, 116
Beech, Hannah, 94
Bengal Renaissance, 31
Bhagavad Gita, 25, 37, 118
Bhakti, 24
Bharatiya Janata Party, 30, 41, 137
Bhishma, 25–6
Bible, 6–7, 30, 72, 99, 117–9, 136
Blacksmith, 46
Bodh Gaya, 46
Bodhi Tree, 46
Bodhisattva, 62, 67, 74, 101
    Kukai, 69
Bodu Bala Sena, 95
Boshin War, 105
Brahman, 19, 23–4, 31, 47, 113–4, 117, 127
Brahmanism, 31
Brahmin, 30, 33, 113
Brahmo Samaj, 31
Brahmoism, 31

155

Index

Brass, Paul, 43, 127–8
Buddha, 44–48, 51–2, 55–6, 58, 63, 66–7, 70, 73–4, 76
   Buddhahood, 46, 61, 66–8
   Shakyamuni, 46, 112, 118
Buddhism Schools, 68
   Nichiren, 68–9, 121
   Pure Land, 68–9, 76
   Shingon, 68–9
   Tendai, 68, 81
   Zen, 13, 51, 53, 68–73, 76, 85–7
Burma, 2, 30, 65, 75, 78, 86, 89–90, 92, 118
Butsudan, 103
Bushido, 71, 86

Camar, 32
Cambodia, 65, 75, 78, 89, 92, 95, 131
Camps, 93
   Detention, 133
   Internment, 133
Caste, 19, 26–7, 30, 32–5, 37, 41, 45, 49, 53, 78, 94, 113, 138
Catholicism, 24, 64, 112, 122
Cavalry, 39
Census, 34, 129
Chen, Quan-quo, 133
China, 2–3, 47–8, 65, 68–70, 75–6, 78, 84–6, 89, 102–3, 108–10, 120–2, 132, 134, 141
Chinese Communist Party, 132–3
Christian Crusades, 134
Christianity, 3, 6–7, 17, 28–9, 31, 53, 58, 75, 78–9, 95–6, 99, 106, 108, 110, 114, 120–1, 123–5, 129–30, 134–6, 139–43, 145
   Negative, 136
   Positive, 136, 143
Citizenship Amendment Bill, 138–9
Class, 33, 68, 70, 85
Code, 98
   *Bu*shido, 71
   Conduct, 37, 54
   Honor, 55, 71
   Monastic, 59, 67
   Samurai, 110
Colonialism, 41, 88, 123
Communism, 89, 93, 122

Communists, 89–90, 93, 109, 133
Conformity, 13, 51
Confucianism, 71, 76–7, 102, 121
Consciousness, 31, 58, 60–4
Constitution, 19–20, 35, 40, 42, 122–3, 139, 143
Cook, Michael, 18–9, 21, 25, 29, 35–6, 115, 125, 137
Corruption, 77, 87
Cosmos, 20, 48, 68
Council, 7, 121
   All Christian Council, 130
   Buddhist, 65, 118
   Great Hindu, 30
   Nicaea, 119
Cows, 19, 39, 127
Cox, Rory, 12
Cosmos, 20, 48, 68
Craving, 58
Cycle, 18–22, 57–61, 93, 113–4

Dalit, 32–3, 138,
Daoism, 47–8, 70, 78, 121–2, 133
Dar al-Harb, 126, 142
Deity, 6, 15, 25–6, 46, 62, 66, 78–9, 101, 106, 116, 127, 145
Delhi Sultanate, 40, 137
Democracy, 35
Demons, 37, 70, 85
Devi, 24, 31
Devotion, 22–4, 52, 62, 113
Dhammapada, 59, 63, 73, 119
Dharma, 11, 18, 20, 23, 26, 29, 46, 48–9, 51, 61–2, 64, 70, 74–5, 80, 82, 85–6, 113, 121
Dharmayuddha, 11, 37
Diplomat, 46
Discipline, 45, 51, 54, 65, 72, 118
Diversity, 16, 29
Doniger, Wendy, 116, 123
Dysentery, 46
Dukkha, 57–8
Dutugamunu, King, 56

Eisai, Priest, 70, 86
Elara, King, 56
Elites, 6, 49

Index

Emperor, 1, 50, 65, 71, 74–7, 102, 104–6, 109, 135–6, 142–3
Empire, 14, 105, 121
　Akkadian, 13
　Assyrian, 13
　Babylonian, 13
　British, 90, 123
　Japanese, 88, 106, 108–9
　Gupta, 25, 68
　Kushan, 75
　Macedonian, 13
　Mauryan, 74
　Meiji, 142
　Mongol, 13
　Mughal, 40, 137
　Ottoman, 13, 40
　Roman, 12–3
　Safavid, 40
　Sumerian, 13
Enlightenment, 46, 53, 55, 60, 64, 70
Epic, 25–6, 38, 124, 126
Equality, 18, 33, 35
Europe, 28, 68, 134–5, 140
Expulsion, 54–5

Facebook, 91
Far East, 3
Fascism, 41
Feudalism, 77
Filipinos, 86
Ford, Eugene, 82
Forest Dweller, 50
Fortifications, 39
Forward Class, 33
Four Noble Truths, 48, 57, 59, 64, 66
Freedom, 18, 35, 60–1, 91, 117, 122, 144
Fronsdal, Gil, 73, 119–20
Fu Jian, 102
Fuehrer, 41
Fundamentalism, 29, 40, 116, 122–5, 136–7, 140
Fundamentalist, 14, 29, 40, 122–3, 136–7
Funerals, 52, 103

Gandhi, Mahatma, 38
Gautama, Siddhartha, 45

Gentiles, 118
Geography, 17–8, 28, 32, 125
Germans, 41, 136
Ghaznavid Kingdom, 76
Gier, Nicholas F., 10–1, 80, 82, 113, 115–6, 118, 126, 140
Gita, 25–6
　Bhagavad, 25, 37, 118
Globalization, 128
God, 6–8, 12–3, 18, 23–6, 29, 31, 47, 79, 98–9. 101, 105, 113, 117, 128, 134, 143,
Gombrich, Richard F., 50, 53, 72, 75, 118, 121
Gopin, Marc, 11
Gort, Jerald, 43
Government, 1–2, 10, 12, 28, 33, 39, 41, 50, 52, 76, 90–3, 106–10, 122, 133–5, 137–9, 143–5
Gravers, Mikael, 95
Great Britain, 19, 37, 88
Great Promulgation Campaign, 107–8
　Great Learning, 107
　Great Teaching, 107
Guam, 2
Gujurat, India, 42, 138
Guru, 68

Hachiman, 101, 103
Hadith, 136
Hague Convention, 144
Hajj, 124
Hall, John, 9
Han, 121, 132–4
Happiness, 19, 58–60, 63
Haraegushi, 100
Hara-kiri, 110
Hardacre, Helen, 101, 105, 109, 111
Harvey, Peter, 56–7, 68
Heaven, 39, 62–3, 69, 98, 101, 121, 143
Hebrew Tribes, 64
Heian Period, 69, 81
Hell, 60, 62–4, 73
Hierarchy, 51, 106–7, 115
Hindi, 18, 28
Hindustan, 28
Hindutva, 27–31, 35, 40–42, 123, 127–30, 136–38, 141, 143

157

Index

Hirohito, Emperor, 86, 109, 135, 140
Hisma, 11
Hitler, Adolph, 136, 140, 143
Holy War, 10, 13–4, 109, 125
Holyland, 28
Human Rights Watch, 43, 124
Huntington, Samuel, 11
Hymns, 21

Ignorance, 58
Impermanence, 58–9
Incest, 56
Indian National Congress, 30, 41
Indonesia, 17, 43, 77, 86, 94
Indus Valley, 39
Infantry, 39
Intent, 18, 51, 63
Intention, 58–9, 63, 85, 142
Intoxication, 57
Iron Age, 72
Ise Grand Shrine, 103, 106
Israel, 7, 10, 64
Italians, 41

Jainism, 17, 34, 47, 49, 78, 112
Jains, 28–9, 139
Jalon, Allan, 87
Jammu, 42
Jataka, 113
Java, 77
Jerryson, Michael, 12, 53, 80–3, 85
Jesus, 6–7, 24, 47, 79, 112, 117–8, 121, 134
Jogye Order, 89
Jones, Jim, 145
Judaism, 3, 6–8, 112, 115, 123, 125
Juergensmeyer, Mark, 11
Jus ad Bellum, 13, 135
Jus in Bello, 13, 135
Just War, 11–3, 37–8, 81, 83, 139

Kamakura Period, 70, 86
Kami, 98–99, 101–3, 114
Kamidana, 103
Kamikaze, 2, 101, 109
Kami-no-Michi, 98
Kandhamal District, 129
Kanishka, the Great, 75

Kannushi, 1
Karma, 18, 22, 55, 59, 61, 63–4, 82, 113
Kar sevaks, 128
Kashmir, 10, 42, 94, 138–9
Kaurava, 25–6
Kegare, 100
Keyes, Charles, 82, 92
King, 10, 13–4, 26, 38, 45, 50, 56, 75–6, 102, 107
Kingdom, 10, 56, 94, 131, 142
  Baekje, 76, 102
  Ghaznavid, 76
  Kalinga, 75
  Kosala, 26
  Kuru, 25
  Saudi Arabia, 137
Kinmei, Emperor, 76, 102
Khmer Rouge, 92
Kittivudho, 89
Kojiki, 100, 102
Kopf, David, 31
Korea, 65, 68, 76–7, 85–6, 89, 102–3, 108, 110, 116, 132, 135
  South, 2–4, 89, 135
  North, 89
Korean War, 85, 139
Koresh, David, 145
Krishna, 23, 26, 38
Kshatriya, 26, 33, 38, 45
Kushan Dynasty/Empire, 75
Kushingar, 46

Lake Baikal, 132
Landlords, 62, 81
Langley, Myrtle, 117
Laos, 65, 78, 89, 93, 95, 131
Laypeople, 52, 61, 84
Lehr, Peter, 13–4, 60, 80, 84–5, 92, 94, 117, 119, 121
Leidig, Eviane, 41
Leninism, 93
Lotus Sutra, 14, 72, 74, 79

MaBa Tha, 96
Mahabharata, 20, 24–6, 37, 124, 141
Mahasabha, 28
Mahasattva, 67

Index

Mahayana, 47, 62, 64–70, 74, 77–8, 81–2, 85–6, 103, 114, 117, 133, 142
Mahendra, 65
Malaysia, 65, 77, 86
Mamluk Dynasty, 40
Manchuria, 86, 108
Mantras, 68
Manusmriti, 20, 27, 32
Mara, 46
Martyrdom, 11
Martyrs, 39
Marx, Karl, 93, 122
Marxist, 93
Mason, JWT, 99, 101
Mauryan, 74
Maya, Queen Maha, 45
Mecca, 7, 123–4
Meditate, 51, 74, 114
Meditation, 46–7, 52, 59, 62, 68, 70, 73
Meiji, 71, 105–9, 142
   Restoration, 105, 142
Mein Kampf, 136
Mendicant, 44
Merit, 22–3, 30, 51, 53, 58, 61–4, 74, 82–3, 107, 113, 135, 143
Middle East, 39, 132, 139
Middle Way, 58
Military, 1–3, 30, 34, 51, 56, 70–1, 74, 77–8, 81, 84–5, 87, 105, 107–8, 110, 120–1, 131, 135, 137, 142, 149
Missionary, 102, 121, 131
Modi, Narenda, 31, 41–2, 130, 138–9
Mohammad, Prophet, 7, 29, 46–7
Monastery, 49, 51–5, 69, 83–4, 90
Money, 23, 50, 53, 57, 100
Mongolia, 65, 68, 76, 78
Monk, 34, 50–4, 78, 82, 84, 91
   Dark, 53
Monotheism, 6
Moon, Reverand, 116
Morality, 55, 59, 62
Moshka, 18, 33
Mosque,
   Al-Aqsa, 7
   Babri, 42, 128

Muslim, 1–4, 16, 39–41, 51, 76–7, 90–2, 94, 115, 121, 16–9, 131–4, 137–40, 142
Myanmar, 2–3, 30, 60, 78, 88–92, 95–6, 131, 139, 142–4
Mythology, 12
Mythohistories, 80
Myths, 6, 11, 24, 41, 96, 102

Nalanda, India, 121
Nationalism, 27–9, 85, 123
Nazis, 136
Nazism, 41
Nelson, John, 101
Nepal, 17, 30, 45, 84
Nicholas II, Tsar, 108
Nihon-gi, 102
Nirvana, 50, 53, 58–61, 64, 66–8, 74, 93
Noble Eightfold Path, 48
Nobles, 38, 117
Norito, 100
Nun, 49–50, 53–59, 62, 76–7

Obedience, 51
Ohnuki-Teirney, Emiko, 103
Olivelle, Patrick, 22
Orders, 35, 48, 109, 119
Ordination, 51
Orrisa, 129
Osama bin Laden, 14
Other Backward Class, 33
Others, 33, 94

Pacific Ocean, 109
Padmasambhava, 68
Pakistan, 2, 30, 42–3, 94, 128, 138–9
Pali, 57
   Canon, 65–6, 71–3, 81, 113, 118
Pandavas, 25
Parrinder, Geoffrey, 75, 115
Parsi, 139
Persecution Relief, 130
Persia, 18, 76
PEW Research Center, 16, 40, 132
Philippines, 86, 110
Philosophers, 12
Pilgrimage, 19, 42, 124
Pillamarri, Akhilesh, 94

Index

Plato, 12
Poem, 25–6, 102
Pogrom, 42, 127–9
Pol Pot, 92
Politician, 28, 47, 50, 128
Polytheism, 6
Pope, 106, 134
Population Control Act, 91
Pork, 46, 51
Port Arthur, 108
Power, 6, 37, 41, 54, 58, 71, 75, 95, 106, 109, 126, 130, 142
  Economic, 43
  Military, 30, 71
  Political, 109, 142
  Spiritual, 98
  State, 20
Precepts, 54, 57
  Five, 54–5
Priest, 1, 7, 48, 52–3, 70, 73, 77, 86–7, 99–100, 103–4, 106–8, 110, 113, 115–6, 118, 135, 142
Prisoners, 38
  Russian, 54
Propaganda, 132–3
Prophet, 6–7, 18, 29, 115, 127
  Mohammad, 7, 29, 46–7
  Muhammad, 6, 46–7, 114, 136–7
Proselytize, 32, 39, 74–5, 120, 126, 134, 142
Protestantism, 44, 64, 112, 121–3, 136
Punjab region, 21
Puranas, 20, 27, 124
Purusha, 32
Pyramid, 33

al-Qaeda, 14, 94, 133, 137
Qing Dynasty, 108
Qur'an, 7, 46, 136

Raj, British, 34, 137
Rajapaksa, Gotabhaya, 95
Rakhine, 90, 92
Rama, 23, 26, 29, 34, 42, 113, 123, 128
Ramayana, 20, 24–6, 37, 141
Rambachan, Anantanand, 16, 36
Rangoon, 89, 118
Rape, 43, 56

Raula, 45
Ravana, King, 26
Rashtriya Swayamsevak Sangh, 30, 40, 137
Rebellions, 77
Rebirth, 16, 18–9, 22–3, 57, 60–3, 67, 73, 93, 113–4, 117
Reincarnation, 55, 59, 62, 78, 113, 135, 143
Reinterpretation, 54, 119
Renunciation, 53, 59
Relics, 47, 56
Rhee, Syngman, 89
Rig Veda, 21–2, 32, 39
Right, 13, 20, 48, 59, 83, 87, 122, 135
  View/Understanding, 58–9
  Intention/Thought, 58–9
  Speech, 58–59
  Action, 58–59
  Livelihood, 58–59
  Effort, 58–9
  Mindfulness, 58–59
  Concentration, 58–9
Riot, 43, 89, 127–9, 138
Roberts, Sean, 134
Rohingya, 2, 90, 92, 139, 144
Roy, Kaushik, 9, 14, 21, 31, 36–7, 83, 112, 120, 126
Royalty, 32, 50
Russia, 68, 108
Russo-Japanese War, 108

Sacrifice, 7, 11, 82
Salvation, 18, 48, 50, 53, 57, 68–9, 121
Sangha, 29, 46, 48–55, 59, 62, 75, 77, 84–90, 92–3, 107, 115, 121
Sanskrit, 11, 18, 20–7, 36, 46, 49, 57, 63, 66–7
Saraswati, Dayananda, 117
Saud, Mohammad bin, 137
Saudi Arabia, 7, 137
Savarkar, Vinayak, 28–30, 39, 43, 136–7, 141
Scheduled Caste/Scheduled Tribes, 33
Schools, 5, 19, 47–9, 54, 62, 64–7, 72, 98, 129
Scripture, 10, 29, 51, 74, 103, 119, 136
Sects, 54, 64, 69, 84–5, 98, 108–9, 126

Index

Secular, 19–20, 28, 30, 40, 76, 123, 139
Secularism, 29, 95, 136
Selengut, Charles, 5–6, 8–10, 13, 122, 125
Seong, Emperor, 76, 102
Sex, 56, 68
Shahada, 7
Shaivites, 31
Shakti, 23, 31
Shakubuku, 121
Shakya Clan, 45
Shaman, 116
Sharma, Arvind, 138
Shingonists, 69
Shinozaki, Michio, 72
Shinto Directive, 110
Shiva, 23–4, 31, 114, 123
Shogunate, 105, 107
Shotoku, Prince, 102
Shrine, 99–100, 103, 105–6, 108–10, 135, 142
Shudra, 32–34
Sikhism, 34, 47, 49, 78, 112
Sikhs, 28–29, 139
Silk Road, 75, 132
Sin, 52, 67, 82–3, 89, 100, 117, 135, 143
Singh, Ameya, 137
Sino-Japanese War
  First, 108
  Second, 109–10
Sita, 26
Slaves, 39, 49, 86
Smith, Huston, 1, 5–6, 44, 47, 79
Sohei, 81
Solar module, 132
Soldiers, 14, 49, 51, 56, 85, 131
Soul, 15, 19, 31, 58, 97, 113
South Asia, 29, 32, 44, 75, 126, 142
Spying, 38
Sramana, 47
Sri Lanka, 3, 65, 72, 75, 78, 85, 88–9, 95, 131
State Shinto, 1–2, 87, 105–10, 135, 142–3
Stockholm Syndrome, 116
Stupas, 47, 52
Suddhodana, King, 45

Suffering, 19, 45–6, 57–8, 60–1, 113, 117
Sufi missionaries, 131
Sufism, 31
Sui, 76, 102
Sumedhananda, 84
Sunni Muslim, 117, 131–3
Sutra, 14, 66–7, 72, 74, 79
Syncretism, 6, 11, 47, 116, 131
Swastika, 136
Sword, 70, 80, 85, 98

Tanaka, 99
Tang Dynasty, 76
Tantra, 31, 68
Temizu, 100
Temple, 7, 18–9, 23–4, 47, 53, 62, 70, 75–6, 81, 83–5, 89, 92–3, 97–9, 103, 107, 114–5, 126, 128, 131, 135, 138
Tendai Tradition, 81
Tennoism, 107
Terrorism, 80, 133
Thailand, 3, 54, 65, 75, 78, 83–6, 88–90, 95, 131
Theism, 6
Theravada, 50, 53, 57, 64–8, 72–5, 78, 81, 90, 95, 117–8, 121, 123–4, 131, 142–3
Thero, Walpola Rahula, 82
Threats, 9–10, 14, 30, 121, 129
Three Jewels, 48, 51
Tibet, 65, 68, 72, 76, 78, 84, 133
Tiele, 132
Tikhonov, Vladimir, 14, 82
Torture, 43, 133
Traders, 74–6, 80, 131
Trimurti, 24
Trinity, 24
Tripitaka, 65, 72–3, 80, 118
Tsumi, 100
Turkestan, 77

Unitarian Universalist Church, 144
United Nations, 2, 91–2, 133
United States, 2–3, 94, 109–10, 133, 138
Universal Life Church, 144

Index

Universe, 22, 24, 31, 48, 99, 113
Upanishads, 18, 20, 22–3, 29, 49, 72, 113, 117–8, 127
Uttar Pradesh, 42
Uyghur, 132–4

Vaishnav, Milan, 29
Vaishnavas, 31
Vaishya, 32–3
Vajpayee, Atal, 129
Vajrayana, 64–5, 68
Varshney, Ashtosh, 28 127–8
Vatican, 134
Veda, 19–22, 25, 28, 32, 39, 49, 102, 112
Vedantism, 31
Vedic, 19–20, 24, 32, 36, 38, 47–8, 63, 117–8
Vegetarians, 51
Victoria, Brian, 53, 71, 77, 87
Vietnam, 65, 68, 86, 89
Vinaya, 54–5, 67
Vishnu, 23–4, 26, 31, 38, 113

Wahhab, Imam, 137
Wahhabism, 137
Wang, Maya, 134

Warfare, Siege, 39
Washington, George, 37
Wen, Emperor, 76
White Anglo-Saxon Protestant, 145
Widows, 35
Wirathu, Ashin, 91–2
Wisdom, 44, 59, 61–2, 67, 98–9
World Health Organization, 9
World War II, 86, 89–90, 109–10, 133, 135, 140, 142–3
Worship, 7, 18, 20, 23–4, 31, 62, 66, 98, 100, 113–5, 122, 124, 135
Wu, Tsung, 76

Xian, 69
Xinjiang, 132–4

Yasukuni Shrine, 110
Yenisei River, 132
Yorktown, Battle, 37
Yoshinobu, Prince Tokugawa, 105
Yu,
   Han, 76
   Xue, 64, 81–2

Zero-sum, 6

www.ingramcontent.com/pod-product-compliance
Lightning Source LLC
Chambersburg PA
CBHW071429160426
43195CB00013B/1851